MIND THE DOORS

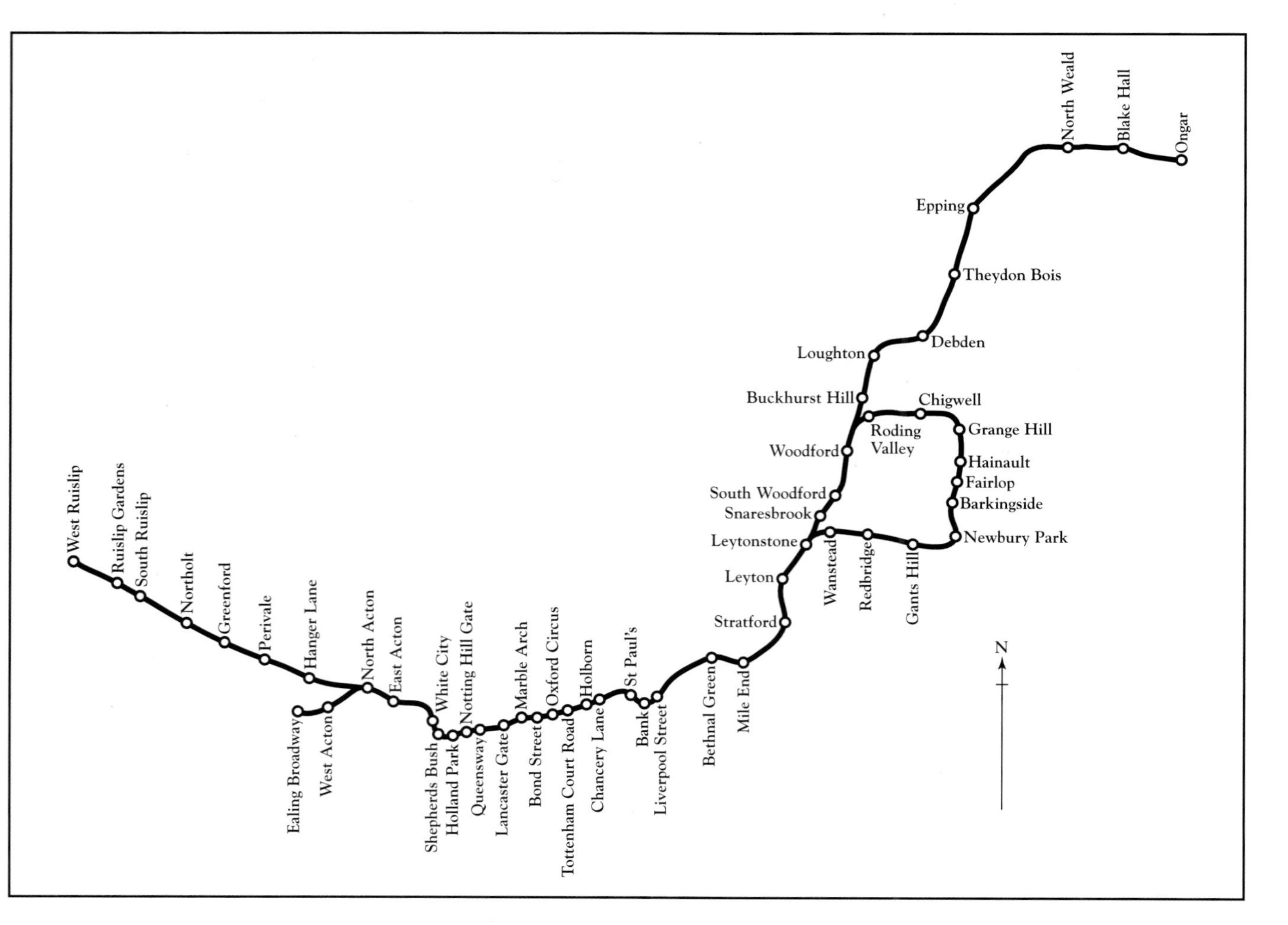

The Central Line

MIND THE DOORS

The life and adventures of a tube train driver

Robert Griffiths

• RAILWAY HERITAGE •

from

The NOSTALGIA *Collection*

ACKNOWLEDGEMENTS

I can only describe my working life on London Underground as unique because of what the job involves, with training, working with other staff, and carrying millions of passengers throughout endless journeys every year.

In the past I have often thought about writing a book concerning my work experience just to prove that driving trains has many responsibilities, more than the average person could ever imagine, especially when safety is involved all the time. So now, after 35 years working on London Underground through different grades, I have plenty to write about my experiences over the years.

I would like to thank my wife, for her support, encouragement and patience, and to my work colleagues Phil Chatfield, Richard Millhouse, Wayne Baker, Dave Fountain, Eddie Walker, Bob Yeldham and many others on London Underground for making the publication of this book possible, not forgetting Peter, Mick and Will from Silver Link Publishing Ltd, for their patience, helpfulness and kindness in helping me achieve my ambition. Also a special thanks to Dianne Millen.

A Silver Link book
from
The NOSTALGIA *Collection*

First published in 2002

British Library Cataloguing in Publication Data

A catalogue record for this book is available from the British Library.

ISBN 1 85794 197 7

Silver Link Publishing Ltd
The Trundle
Ringstead Road
Great Addington
Kettering
Northants NN14 4BW

Tel/Fax: 01536 330588
email: sales@nostalgiacollection.com
Website: www.nostalgiacollection.com

Printed and bound in Great Britain

All photographs are by the author unless otherwise credited.

CONTENTS

A driver's eye view of the Central line: approaching Queensway station westbound. *R. Millhouse*

INTRODUCTION

I was born in the quaint old town of Epping in Essex, after the war years in 1948. As I was one of twins, with an older sister too, we were an average family, fairly poor, living in an old terraced house in a cul-de-sac backing on to the Central Line.

My parents worked very hard to give us what they could afford. Admittedly, we didn't get as much as we might have wished, but on the whole we were a very happy family – contented with what we had, never taking anything for granted, and accepting our lives the way they were, because we'd never known it any other way. Schooling was a top priority. My parents wanted us to get as much education as possible. Although I was never a top scholar nor sat in the higher-grade classrooms, at least I got enough of an education to set me up for my future.

In my younger days, what with living so near to the Central Line, I began to take an interest in railways, like most young boys. I would often stand on the footbridge, waving to the drivers in their silver 1959 tube-trains, thundering down the line. The drivers would wave back, sounding the train whistle to acknowledge my excitement.

Often my parents would send me to the goods yard at Epping station to buy a sack of coal, which I used to load into my four-wheeled trolley. This was my favourite errand and took me longer than expected, as I used to stand and watch the old steam locomotives shunting the coal wagons back and forth into the sidings. I would also watch them turn on the large turntable, getting ready for their return journey to Stratford, where they would fetch more coal to serve Epping. I can vaguely remember travelling from Epping to Ongar by steam locomotive on this Essex branch line before 1957. The engine was a Holden 2-4-2, working a push-pull service until electrification was extended to the end of the line on 18 November 1957. After that the steam locos were replaced with tube-trains.

To travel on the underground was a very rare treat in my younger days – we only went when my parents took us sightseeing in London. I shall always remember what my father used to tell us when we entered the tunnel sections: you must swallow to prevent your ears blocking up with the air pressure in the tunnel. I was very impressed with the underground system, more so than with the actual sights in London.

Once my school days were over it was time to face the big wide world. I felt very unsure of employment. Admittedly, I had lots of choice because there were plenty of vacant positions in those days, even for people like me, without qualifications. However, working on the railway never entered my mind at the time, because as I got older I had other interests – there was so much going on.

My first job – learning how to become a tailor – only lasted for six months. I was cutting out material to make ties, but I wasted so much material, being unable to cut straight, that the company decided it would be cheaper for them to sack me. My second job, which lasted for a year this time, was packing eggs. I worked in an old pre-war factory that had been used as an army camp in the Second World War. I must admit that standing at the end of a long conveyor-belt packing eggs into large boxes wasn't very exciting. Saturdays used to be overtime days, when I could volunteer to wash down the lorries in the yard to earn extra wages. I decided to leave after a year because the company moved to Stansted in Essex and that was too far to travel each day.

My third job was as a trainee painter and decorator. At least with this job, I thought, I could learn a trade that would be useful later on in life. The company gave me a choice between becoming an apprentice or just carry on working as normal, and I declined the apprenticeship because my salary would have been much lower. I soon began to settle down and enjoy this new job. It taught me so much, especially when it came to doing private jobs to earn extra money to make up for the poor salary (£10 a week).

In that year – 1965 – my twin brother and I formed a pop group. He played drums and I played the bass guitar, despite the fact that neither of us had any musical knowledge. Once our pop group began to sound a bit more musical we played at local venues, putting up with the girls screaming at us. I grew my hair long to look more fashionable, like the Beatles and the Rolling Stones, and it was great to feel famous and be noticed, signing autographs and arranging dates with the female fans – until I met my future wife.

I was made redundant from my painting and decorating job when the company went bust, so I was again searching for employment until my uncle, who was a train driver, mentioned that there were vacant positions on the underground. At first I declined because I couldn't imagine working in such a vast system surrounded by millions of passengers every day. Admittedly, my boyhood ambition had been to become a train driver, but as you grow up your mind turns to other things, as daily life takes over. However, eventually I decided to give London Underground a try. If I didn't like this new experience, I could always find employment elsewhere, after all.

Now it seems as if my working life has gone past very quickly, with only another 13 years to go before retirement. I have made many friends over the years among my railway colleagues. Many have retired, died, resigned or taken promotion to other lines. Having been involved with many operating problems including signal failures, train breakdowns, strange passenger behaviour and suicides, I have had plenty of experience as a qualified train driver to keep the wheels turning for the future.

1
GOING UNDERGROUND

It was 1966. England had just won the World Cup, the Beatles were top of the charts, and I was about to experience being made redundant from my job. After searching through countless newspapers for job vacancies, I decided to join London Transport, giving in to my interest in railways.

The morning of my interview I felt very nervous. In fact, my whole body was shaking like a leaf. Having been raised in rural Essex, I wasn't used to crowds of people, and I certainly needed a map and compass to find my way around. When I arrived for my interview at Griffith House I was told to wait in the interview room surrounded by other new recruits of all different nationalities. My twin brother kept me company, because he wanted to follow in my footsteps.

Suddenly my surname was called out in a very loud voice. I walked into the interview room – still shaking like a leaf – to face a rather stern-looking interviewer. After answering many personal questions, I was told to wait in the dull-looking waiting room while my twin brother was being interrogated. Once all of the new recruits had been interviewed, we all took the simple aptitude test. I had never been too bright and I'd been dreading this part of the process all along. Perhaps I should have listened to my teacher more at school and got more out of my education. But it was too late for regrets. I was one of the last to finish and the results looked poor. To add to my misery, I couldn't cheat by peering at my brother's answers because each desk was set apart.

However, once all the test papers had been marked, to my great surprise I found that I had been accepted. My brother was told to re-apply at a later date over some confusion with his previous employer. I wanted to be a Guard, but unfortunately all the vacancies for this were filled, giving me very little choice other than to become a railman working on the stations.

My next task was the medical, but that didn't bother me as I was quite fit and healthy in my younger days. I particularly used to enjoy cross-country running and gymnastics at school. I did go through one stage standing on my head a lot, something else I used to enjoy; I know it takes all sorts to make a world, and at least it made a change from standing on my feet. The medical was pretty straightforward, just to make sure you were fit enough without any health problems. I shall always remember the doctor looking down my Y-fronts and telling me to cough. I passed my medical with flying colours and was very pleased to have got that far; some applicants had failed their aptitude tests and others their medicals.

After lunch we received our free staff travel passes and a welcome booklet describing the history of London Transport. Now I had been accepted, I began to wonder where my future working location would be. I didn't want to spend long hours travelling to and from work, especially in the early hours of the morning or late at night. At the time I didn't realise that London Transport ran trains and buses specially for their staff.

Next we were taken to Chiswick Works in an old RT double-decker bus, and when we arrived we were taken to the uniform clothing store to be measured up. I had to accept whatever I was given nearest to my size, as nothing was tailor-made. Standing there in my black uniform overcoat, the hem inches from the ground, I must have looked just like an undertaker! This was the smallest size they had. It's just as well I wasn't any shorter, otherwise I would have had to become a road sweeper. My uniform trousers were a bit baggy as well – from behind I looked like the Elephant Man, as the crotch had plenty of room. Perhaps this is a slight exaggeration, but I had been used to wearing the tight-fitting, modern clothes of the 1960s.

Outside the uniform store we were greeted by trade union representatives. They reminded me of Jehovah's Witnesses, standing there with their briefcases handing out pieces of paper to us new recruits. We had to join a union in those days, which meant we had a very hard choice between ASLEF and the NUR. My knowledge of unions was non-existent, and most of us chose to join the cheapest one – I for one was hard up for money, having been out of work for a few weeks and practically down to my last penny.

Once again it was time to board the old RT bus, and our destination this time was White City Training School, where they would teach us how to become railmen. So far I was impressed with how much we had achieved in one day. With only an hour or so to go before it was time to head for home, we were given a lecture about what was expected from us. At least by now I was no longer shaking like a leaf and the worse was over for one day. However, I was still feeling unsure if this job was right for me, although at least my future employment was going to be completely different from painting and decorating. The salary was much higher as well, and we would be earning double-time on Sundays. The financial side of my life was going to improve, providing I didn't waste my money on silly things.

I have to admit that at the time I couldn't save money no matter how hard I tried. I always owed my parents money because my week's salary would only last a few days. At 18 years of age, spending money like water didn't bother me at all. I had nothing to save up for, after all.

The next morning I struggled out of bed for my first day of learning my railman's job at the training centre. It was like being back at school, sitting behind a desk, although at least you were allowed to smoke – anti-smoking rules didn't exist in those days. If we wanted to use the loo, we had to put up our hands and ask if we could be excused. Our Training Instructors seemed to be very strict. Lateness would not be tolerated in any way – you had to have a good excuse for being late or you got an excessive telling-off – and if lateness became a habit you would soon be looking elsewhere for employment. We had to respect our Instructors if we wanted a career with London Transport, even if we detested them.

Our first day was spent learning rules and regulations, and we were each given a rule-book, which became our bible. The rule-book was a hardback volume in large print. Most of the rules were out-dated, because steam trains didn't run in passenger service and were only used in the depots for shunting until they were scrapped altogether. Some rules had been in existence since the underground was created, but there was no reason to change them because time stood still on the underground. It was always a very long time before changes were made.

The rules and regulations also included how signals work, and these were quite easy if you were electrically minded, as we had to learn the wiring circuit as well. Once you understood the basics, the rest was only common sense. Learning how the traction current was fed into the running and current rails from the sub-stations was very interesting – I was beginning to take an interest, which helped my learning ability to improve to the satisfaction of the Instructors. There was much to learn and the weeks ahead seemed never-ending.

With so much to be learned from hand-outs, films and verbal instruction, you would often feel tired, especially by the end of the week. If you dozed off in class you were guaranteed to be woken up by a flying blackboard rubber. Instructors would not tolerate this behaviour – it proved you were either bored with the lesson or bored with the Instructor, and tiredness was considered no excuse. I was beginning to think I had joined

The White City Training School, now disused. The new training school is at South Kensington, known as Ashfield House. Local training of train crews is mainly done at depots.

the Army! The training centre had a mock-up platform that helped with the practical side of learning, while the classroom lessons dealt with the theory. Station training was very important even before you stepped on to a platform to face the passengers and the many operating problems that could occur.

A few weeks later we new recruits were released from the training school, and the feeling of freedom was wonderful. I was sent to Oxford Circus station, and felt like a clown because I was completely lost in the many miles of subways, and dreaded passengers asking for directions. Oxford Circus was an interchange station between the Bakerloo and Central Lines; in addition, the Victoria Line was nearing completion and opened a year later. My first lesson in station training was to scrub from the tiles the dry paste left by the billposters. I thought I had made a good job of it until I was told to do it again. I started to feel discontented, like a glorified cleaner in uniform.

Standing on the platform shouting 'Mind the doors!' was embarrassing at first until I got used to it. Often passengers got trapped in the train doors after you warned them that they were closing. At first I blamed myself for this, thinking I should have given them time to board the train. But if I had given them time, the train would have been delayed, as the flow of passengers was endless. I wasn't too happy working on the busy underground stations, and would have preferred a quieter life working on open-section stations in the fresh air.

My first day working at Oxford Circus was a complete nightmare. I made a cock-up of everything I did. A young lady standing on the platform waiting to go home decided to faint, and passengers looked to me to do something, as I was the clown in uniform. Not knowing where the telephone was to call the Stationmaster, I ran up the long escalator to seek help from a member of staff – I had no knowledge of first aid in my younger days. By the time I arrived back on the platform with another member of staff, the young lady had fully recovered to continue her journey.

At long last my station training at Oxford

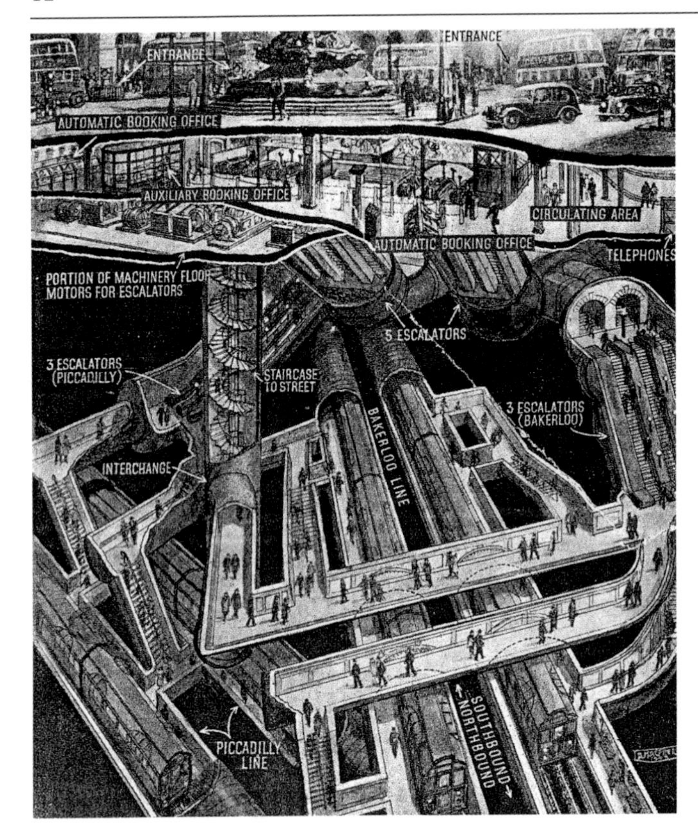

I was completely lost in the many miles of subways at Oxford Circus station, as can be appreciated from this cutaway view of Piccadilly Circus, another important interchange station on the network. *R. Macpherson, from Odhams' Railways, Ships and Aeroplanes Illustrated*

Circus came to an end, and it was time to go back to the training centre to see how every new recruit had got on in his or her training. At least I had become a professional scrubber, and an athlete from running up the escalators. The training school received written reports from the Stationmasters with whom we had done our station training; all of us passed this stage, and to our relief we learned that we were now professional station cleaners and platform attendants. However, there was still plenty to learn in this grade, and only experience would help to give us that.

My home life, with my parents, two brothers and sister, was very hectic considering I was on shift work. My mother used to pull her hair out because the family could never sit down together at the dinner table. I used to prefer the early shifts because the pop group that my brother and I had formed practised in the evenings and played at local dance-halls and clubs. Luckily, back then I could get away with only four hours' sleep without feeling too tired the next day.

I began to feel proud in my black uniform despite the long overcoat and having to wear a cap with my long hair. The uniform jacket and overcoat had yellow piping around the collar and cuffs, and the lapels bore the hand-sewn 'griffin' emblem that symbolised London Transport. The uniform was very heavy to wear although it was long-lasting. I must have looked quite comical, with my 'winkle-picker' boots and my long hair hanging down from inside my cap. My Stationmaster often dropped hints that I should get my hair cut, but I ignored him as I wanted to keep in fashion.

When I first joined London Transport the tube-trains on the Central Line were only four years old and were very reliable, giving the Central Line the best record of service compared to the other lines on the network. The Northern Line was always called the 'misery line' because the equipment was so old it continually broke down. The 1959 stock on the Central Line had replaced the Standard stock, which had also been very reliable in its day, lasting for 24 years. It looked very modern, and was painted silver, giving it an elegant appearance. The interior, with its shiny wooden floors and red-upholstered seats, also certainly made this tube-train stand out from the rest of the London Transport fleet. It was replaced by the 1962 stock, which was very similar, and most of the 1959 stock was transferred to the Piccadilly line.

Once all my station training and assessments had been completed, I was ready to be let loose on a station. I was praying that they wouldn't give me Oxford Circus or some other busy underground station because of my training experience, but Lady Luck must have been looking down on me that day, for I was sent to Loughton in Essex on the Central Line. This station suited me down to the ground, as it was on an open section station without subways, escalators or lifts.

Stationed at Loughton I became a 'Rest day cover Railman', which meant that I had to cover a group of stations at the eastern end of the Central Line. It also meant that I could cover for a Station Foreman or Ticket Collector on my spare days. I thought this was absurd because these grades were higher than Railman, and I had no training whatsoever to enable me to do their jobs. I was thrown in at the deep end, but slowly learned about these grades from experience.

My first task on early shifts was to wash out the public toilets. I hated this job as it made me feel very embarrassed. My other cleaning jobs were to polish all the brasswork and to sweep and wash all the floors in the station premises. I did platform duties in the rush hour, followed by more station cleaning until it was time to go home. Admittedly, I had a very cushy job and was beginning to enjoy every minute of it. My work colleagues seemed very friendly and gave me many useful tips, making my station working much easier to cope with. The only thing I disliked was my spare days when I was often sent to a busy underground station to cover staff absence. Eventually I got used to the crowds of passengers and learning my way through miles of subways, where the buskers sang and played.

One morning I had to cover staff sickness at St Paul's station. My grade that day was collecting tickets – something of which I had little experience. Standing in the ticket collector's box I was astounded and horrified to see so many passengers. I had to collect every ticket that was handed to me, and collect excess fares, which I had to write down on a sheet, stating the time. I had problems trying to keep up with the never-ending surge of passengers, making me feel dizzy. A member of staff who at first laughed at me eventually came to my rescue. Perhaps I did look silly covered in tickets and surrounded by lots of money.

Fares from passengers and the booking office revenue used to be stored in a secret stronghold room on the station, then we railmen used to load the bags of money on to a four-wheeled trolley and push it along the street to the bank. This practise ceased once London Transport hired security firms. I can't recollect any incidents of robbery when shifting money in this way, but at least the modern method was safer for everyone concerned.

My first year working for London Transport had passed very quickly. My twin brother was now a signalman at North Weald on the Central Line, and he enjoyed his cushy job pulling the long levers in the old wooden signal box. My father also enjoyed his job as a bus conductor at Loughton, and my mother was now coping very well with our shift work. However, the pop group began to split up because the other members began to get fed up with our shifts. Many of our bookings had to be cancelled, and eventually the group came to an end.

At Loughton I was given a nomination form to select the stations at which I wanted to work. I only selected a few stations, all in the open sections that I liked the best – I enjoyed the quite life, and who could blame me? I wanted to settle down working at one station only rather than all over the place, and certainly didn't want to work on busy underground stations for the same salary as I got at Loughton.

Often I felt ashamed to tell my friends outside the job that I cleaned stations, because it sounded as if I was just a cleaner. Although it was only a cleaner's job in a way, it also involved platform duties, helping passengers and assisting train crews, for example telephoning the Line Controller for them if they were experiencing problems.

One Sunday I was sent to Theydon Bois to cover staff sickness, thinking I was going to have a nice easy day because this station was very quite at the weekends. However, the Station Foreman, who reminded me of a sergeant-major, sat in the ticket collector's box all through his shift, and I felt very awkward because there wasn't much to do as far as cleaning was concerned; it could be completed in an hour, as the station was clean anyway. The Foreman watched every move I made, ensuring I was doing my cleaning jobs correctly. When I completed my station duties early, he sent me out to the car park to pick up every piece of litter I could find.

Most Station Foremen were really great to work under, however. Some didn't bother too much about the station duties, just as long as you were there and made some effort. Sometimes they used to send you home early, providing the service was running as normal and they had enough staff to cope if an emergency did arise.

2
RODING VALLEY

Now with two years experience, I was sent to Fairlop station, which was the first time I had worked there. At least it was an open-section station, so I had no escalators and lifts to worry about and no more crowds of passengers to contend with. The Station Foreman was OK, providing my station duties were completed to his satisfaction; often he ran out of pipe tobacco, forcing him to smoke tea-leaves in his pipe. The cleaning duties were practically non-existent – there was very little to do because the station was so quiet and had very few buildings. The group Stationmaster paid a visit every day to sign the log-book, and this was one time when you had to look busy to keep out of trouble.

One evening a group of troublesome youths vandalised the station, breaking windows in the telephone kiosk on the platform. The police were called quickly and arrested the youths, and much to my disgust I had to attend court as a witness. The youths were fined and never came back to Fairlop station. This was my first taste of vandalism on the railway.

My training at the school went satisfactorily – at least I knew all about tickets and season tickets, more than I had done before. Now I was a qualified Ticket Collector, collecting tickets to my heart's content. Being qualified made me feel more relaxed; at least I could tell the difference between the various types and could look for outdated and forged tickets from the passengers. Often passengers would quickly flash their season tickets in front of your eyes, while others quickly threw their tickets into the ticket box to make their hasty escape. All this changed when the Ticket Inspectors invaded the stations, and many fiddling passengers found themselves going to court for fare evasion.

In my leisure time I was falling in love. My girlfriend was very special and I had chased her for months to get a date. I had finally convinced her that I was her prince, if not in shining armour then in a long black overcoat. She was still at school, only 14 years of age and very pretty, with long fair hair and blue eyes. We kept our dates to a minimum because she wasn't allowed to stay out late. With her mum's permission, I was allowed to take her to the cinema at least once a week, providing it was the weekend or during the school holidays.

Another year passed, and I was becoming fed up working at Fairlop station – there was nothing there to get excited about, and the novelty was wearing off. Every day was the same without much to do – the other staff felt the same way because it was just too quiet. Once again I was transferred to another open-section station, Roding Valley, which was just as quiet as my previous one but with one big difference – the staff were much friendlier, giving the station a happy atmosphere.

Once again I was sent to the training school, this time to learn how to use the 'Gibson Ticket Machine', the same as that used by bus conductors; Roding Valley station was the only station on the entire transport system that used one. It was great fun reeling off the tickets to the passengers, as well as collecting tickets at the same time. I still had my station cleaning duties to do, which I didn't mind. We kept our station as clean as a

Roding Valley, the first station on the Hainault loop. This now the only unmanned station on the Central Line.

whistle, feeling proud of the clean platforms, shining brasswork, polished floors and gleaming windows.

I had begun writing lyrics as a new hobby, mainly concerned with love, as I was a romantic then. One day one of our passengers came on to the station with his guitar. I showed him my lyrics and he was so impressed that he started writing the music for them. One song I wrote nearly got published after I signed a contract with a music publisher in London. London Transport got to hear about it (not knowing that we used the staff mess room as a recording studio after the rush hour had passed), and the following week I was having my photograph taken for the staff magazine. My songs never did get published, however, and it seemed like a waste of time and money. I even had two demo records made at a recording studio, but the only result was to empty my bank account and shatter my dreams once more. The photograph didn't get published either. I was told it was because of my long hair – perhaps I looked a disgrace in those days! They did write a very good article about my songs, however, so at least if I wasn't to become famous I felt very famous for a time.

To make my life exciting once again I decided to take up a new hobby – gardening. I had plenty of spare time to cultivate the station garden at Chigwell, which was the next station from Roding Valley on the Woodford to Hainault loop line. I found gardening very hard work, starting from scratch, but once I had made a fishpond out of plastic, and bought turf and plants, I was amazed at the difference from when I had first started. The first year I received a Third Class award, followed by a First Class award the following year. Often I would pick a bunch of flowers to give to my girlfriend, not realising that dahlias attracted earwigs, only for my future mother-in-law to watch them crawling over her carpets.

When I finally got engaged to my girlfriend, and marriage was on the cards, we decided to go house-hunting. We couldn't afford a high mortgage because of our low salaries – my girlfriend was now working in a shoe shop full time, and saving like mad. I was doing my best

Cultivating my award-winning station garden at Chigwell. My efforts were rewarded by a Third Class award for the first year.

1960 Craven tube stock as modified for automatic train operation, working on the Hainault loop line.
A. Rogers

to save as well, even though it was a terrible struggle. The mortgage we could afford bought us a run-down uninhabitable cottage in Loughton, and we had one year to modernise it before we got married. It was great fun putting my non-existent DIY skills to the test. Our neighbours nearly called out the fire brigade one night after I accidentally set light to an old air-raid shelter; lucky for me I got hold of a hosepipe very quickly to put out the flames.

At about this time London Transport used the Woodford to Hainault loop line to test-run the automatic trains for the Victoria Line, which was already up and running, having opened in 1968. London Transport had converted its 'Craven stock' into automatic trains, and further tests had to be completed to amend the first teething problems on trains and coding. Once it was satisfied with the running of the Victoria Line, London Transport decided to keep the Craven stock running on the Hainault loop. This type of automatic system was superb, doing London Transport credit.

Tube-trains running on the open sections of line suffered problems with ice and snow, primarily with the positive and negative pick-up shoes, and the current rails had difficulty conducting the 650 volts under such conditions. Sometimes a push from another train was recommended, providing it didn't get stuck as well. The driver had to use his ice-scraper to scrape the rails, often under appalling weather conditions. When bad weather was forecast, London Transport used to run a converted 1939/40 'sleet train', which sprayed de-icing fluid on to the rails and also had brushes to get the ice and snow off the live rails.

My Stationmaster suggested I should consider promotion to become a Guard. At first I declined because I was very happy and contented on the station – we were one big happy family sharing our lives together and enjoying much fun and laughter, not forgetting the song-writing and gardening. We also shared our pleasure with most of the passengers, who had time to talk to us. I had never known such a friendly atmosphere on the railway before. However, I knew I needed to go for promotion in order to earn more money for my forthcoming marriage. When all was said and done, I couldn't be expected to work on this station for the rest of my life, especially when there was the chance to earn more money.

I prevaricated for ages, but my Stationmaster wouldn't take no for an answer until I gave in to his request. Then every day he would teach me about train equipment, which at first I found very hard to digest; it all seemed very complicated and there was too much to learn. I began to have my doubts about promotion and to feel very disheartened. My Stationmaster even took me to Hainault depot and showed me underneath a train that was stabled on a shed road. Now I started to become more interested and begun to understand my studies a bit more.

Having applied for promotion, the only setback to my plans was the need to wait for the training school to call me; as there was little demand for new guards, I could be waiting for at least another year. Still, I was contented working on the station, and didn't mind the long wait. At least it gave me time to study all the more, and understand what I was learning. I did find a lot of it very difficult, especially the braking system, with so many positions to learn. I tried not to learn it parrot fashion, as this was easily done until someone asked you 'Why?'. 'Why' was the horrible word everyone hated. If you could not explain the answer correctly, it proved that you only knew something parrot fashion rather than understanding it properly.

While I was waiting for promotion I was very busy in my spare time. I was still modernising my old run-down cottage, hoping that it would soon be suitable to live in. The summer months were spent attending to the station garden at Chigwell, preparing for my next prizes. My average night's sleep was only about four hours and I wished there were more hours in the day. On late shifts I hardly saw my girlfriend apart from my rest days. I therefore decided to give up my station garden at Chigwell, somewhat against my will, but at least it would give me more time to modernise our future home in Loughton.

The train I hated the most: 'Sleet' locomotive ELS 907, now on display at Acton Museum. *C. Richard*

With all the laughter and pranks we used to get up to on the station, everyone was horrified to hear that one of the staff had passed away after a sudden heart attack in the night. He was the type who always made everyone laugh at him, and the passengers adored and admired him for his cheeky cheerfulness. Most of the staff attended his funeral, and everyone followed the hearse in their cars, only to discover to their horror that we were at the wrong cemetery. 'Polly', as he was nicknamed, was the type of person who would play this prank, whether dead or alive.

My last few months working on the station before returning to the training school drew nearer. I felt I was now ready to face the task of becoming a guard. And if I was going to fail, at least I would be returning to my station.

One day my Stationmaster sent me on the Piccadilly Line to meet one of his friends who was a train driver. I spent nearly the whole day in the driver's cab, learning everything about trains. This experience made me feel keener than before to work on the train side. The driver even let me drive the train in between stations to get the feel of things, and I enjoyed every minute of the experience.

Before being accepted into the training school, I was interviewed by one of our managers, who asked me many questions about train equipment. Luckily I had studied beforehand and gave him more correct answers than wrong ones, and this successful interview brought me closer to my training course.

My very last week working on the station before beginning my training arrived. One morning in the rush hour, when a busy train arrived at the station, there was sudden panic among the passengers in one of the carriages. To our horror we found a male passenger dead on the floor, and we carried him off the train before the medics arrived. I felt completely sick knowing that I had touched a dead body – this was my first experience of this type of horror. The rest of the day I couldn't eat. Even my hands felt waxy with the thought of it.

In five years of station working I had experienced a lot. Perhaps in the beginning I had thought that I was only a glorified cleaner in uniform, but now my duties were to assist in ticket collecting, platform duties and giving passengers directions. Another job was the filling of the stoplights in the sidings with paraffin. I wasn't going to miss a lot of the station duties, especially emptying litterbins, washing out toilets and cleaning up vomit from late-night travellers who had drunk too much. My stomach could never take such things, and I was very surprised and occasionally sickened to see what passengers threw away in litterbins. However, station working had been easy compared with the two jobs I had done before joining London Transport, especially when I had got on well with the staff with whom I had to work.

At long last I was told to attend the training centre one Monday morning. I felt very nervous and wanted to change my mind, but I couldn't let down my Stationmaster now because he had tried his best to help me get on. I appreciated him very much and respected his kindness.

3
PROMOTION TO GUARD

Monday morning soon arrived for the 30 students at the training school. Our first week was to involve being taught rules and regulations from scratch. With only one week to digest it all, I nevertheless felt quite at ease because I had already done some of the work. Some of the students were direct recruits, giving me an advantage over them in the learning procedure.

Our classroom contained a large model train set, with model trains very similar to those in use on the District Line. It was there to show students how trains kept their distance from each other on a running line, and also to explain methods in signalling and other procedures that would be covered in our studies.

In our first week we had lots of writing to do, mainly copying from the blackboard. Often in lessons we would be asked a question out of the blue, just to keep us on your toes and make sure we hadn't nodded off. I found it very tiring sitting in the classroom, especially when I knew the answers anyway.

After rules and regulations it was time to find the weakest links among the students. Each of us had to sit an oral examination covering everything we had been taught, and some students failed with very low marks, although they were invited to return to the training centre in the near future. The lucky ones amongst us that passed had next to face the nightmare of learning train equipment.

The following Monday morning we all met in the staff canteen, waiting to be shown to the train equipment room. This was very large, since arranged down one side of it was actual train equipment. The room next door contained a mock-up of a train carriage so that we could learn the door procedures of a tube train. In the corner stood the famous blackboard with its flying blackboard rubber for dozing students.

I was very surprised to learn that guards had to know quite a bit about train equipment and train defects. This was going to be a very tough week for everyone, with plenty of concentration needed for school and homework. During our train equipment training we were given a lot of hand-outs concerning train defects. One was quite comical, showing a cartoon character called 'Motorman Percy'. At least this cheered up the students as the classroom echoed with laughter. 'Motorman Percy' was a train driver with no forward movement on his train. The cartoon sketches showed him going through each procedure until he succeeded in moving his train.

That second week went very quickly, although I was suffering from continuous headaches and sleep deprivation due to homework, which was optional but necessary if you fell behind with the lessons. Admittedly I still felt confused over some things, but at least I wasn't the only student who felt that way.

After a nice, long relaxing weekend, I was sent to Loughton depot to gain experience on a train in passenger service. My first few days were spent with a trainer guard, learning how to open and close the doors. I wasn't too keen on the rush hour until I had got the hang of the passenger flow, enabling me to judge when to close the doors without causing delay or injury to passengers.

My next big step was to drive a train – this was the moment I had been waiting for. Luckily, the trainer was my uncle. I felt like a big kid, driving along with a huge grin on my face – until I overran a station! My biggest challenge was holding down the 'dead man's handle', a safety device that, if released, due to sudden illness, for example, would cause the train to stop. My hands and wrist ached until pins and needles took effect. Feeling a little nervous, but excited too, it was a great experience (although nobody knew it was actually my second time!). Guards had to learn to drive a train in case their driver collapsed while on duty. The guard was only allowed to drive it to the next station or the nearest depot or siding before another driver would take over.

After my excitement of driving trains, it was back to the training school for the dreaded oral examination. To cut a long story short, I passed with flying colours. Some students failed, although they were allowed to sit their examinations again after a few days of refresher courses.

My days working on stations had now come to an end, and I was a qualified guard, albeit one with little experience. I was stationed at Loughton depot on the Central Line with my uncle, who taught me the tricks of the trade about jobs that required some skill. I had already met the drivers and guards when I worked at Loughton as a railman. Many drivers were getting on a bit and had worked for many long years on the underground. They seemed to be very friendly and good to work with, although a few of them admitted that they didn't like guards because they thought they were higher in grade than they were.

Before I could perform my duties I needed to be issued with equipment from the running office. This consisted of notebook, pencil, cloth, hand-lamp, timetable, equipment bag and a guard's position key. The latter looked like a large spanner which was placed into the barrel of the control panel to operate the train

Both ends of the underground section of the Central Line: a driver's view of the tunnel mouth at Leyton in the east, and a train of 1962 tube stock emerging from the tunnel at White City in the west. *R. Millhouse*

doors. I had to buy a large tea-can as well, as making tea was very important to your driver. You weren't considered a proper guard unless you could make a can of tea; the driver and guard took it in turns to make it, either on the road or at meal breaks.

Although I had been fitted out with all my equipment, I was still not quite ready to be let loose at the back of the train. I spent the next few days hiking around all the depots and sidings. Ruislip depot was the worst, stretching for at least a mile with many roads on which to stable your train. Even to this day I still get confused on some roads, especially in the sheds. My last task was to pass out in front of a Divisional Manager, showing him that I could operate the train doors and drive a train in passenger service using two different braking systems.

On my first proper day as a Guard I felt very nervous, although my driver was only eight carriages away if I needed help. I had no trainer to keep an eye on me, so I just had to do my best. Admittedly, I was very slow closing the train doors because I didn't want to trap any passengers; if the driver thought I was too slow, he would notch the train up to make it jolt. Some drivers understood what I was going through. Others were only interested in keeping to time and didn't care about the poor guard at the back of the train. However, after a few weeks of experience I began to settle down and was able to move much more quickly without catching passengers in the doors, unless it was their own silly fault, of course. My pet hate was when passengers held the doors open with their briefcases or umbrellas, in order to try and board the train once the doors were closing.

By July 1972 my old terraced house was completely modernised, and fit for a Queen to live in! I got married in Epping, Essex, the home town of both my wife and myself, and the wedding went without a hitch as expected. We spent a two-week honeymoon at Butlin's holiday camp at Bognor Regis, then returned home to move into our own house at last.

There were extensive and bewildering stabling sidings at Ruislip depot, as this photograph shows. In the foreground is a train of withdrawn 1962 tube stock awaiting its fate.

For a while when I got back to work I was teased by my work colleagues, who expected me to book on in the mornings with bleary eyes, looking half-asleep. Booking on for duty in the early hours of the morning was a killer unless you went to bed early. I hated early shifts after a while; you were always tired and never felt like doing anything at home, except sleeping for an hour or so. Being a guard wasn't itself hard work – in fact it was very cushy and relaxing. Travelling to work was more tiring than anything else.

Spare duties on the rota consisted of standing spare to cover for staff sickness. Providing all the train crews came in to work, my spare day was a doddle; as long as you stayed on the premises, you could do what you liked up to a point – ideal for washing the car, playing darts or playing cards.

Worst of all were the split duties, consisting of a 12-hour day. Admittedly, you only worked eight of the hours, but even so it was very tiring by the end of the week. Night duties were very cushy, given that train crews had at least four hours of rest during the night. Of course the split and night duties paid the highest salary, and working double-time on Sundays certainly brought in the cash.

Six months passed very quickly, I was settling in very well and enjoying my guard's job. The next promotion was to go back to the training school and become a train driver. I didn't feel ready for this – I had hardly any experience as a guard, let alone being ready for the responsibility of driving trains. I failed my oral examination because I found it very hard to understand the train equipment, about which drivers had to learn more than guards.

In 1974 my wife gave birth to our daughter. Now my life was falling into place and I felt great happiness and contentment. My twin brother took promotion to Station Foreman and was stationed at Debden. My Father resigned from his bus conductor's job when London Transport closed down Loughton bus garage, and took up caretaking for a local school in Epping.

Friday 28 February 1975 – no train driver will ever forget the Moorgate crash on the Northern & City branch. Train 272 from Drayton Park depot had already completed several return trips to and from Moorgate, and when it departed from Drayton Park at 8.39am everything seemed quite normal. However, as the train approached platform 9 at Moorgate in the busy morning rush hour, gaining speed up to 40mph, the horrified passengers and staff realised that it wasn't going to stop. There was nothing they could do as the train hit the red stop lamp with its single hydraulic buffer beyond and crashed into the tunnel wall.

Forty-two passengers and the driver were killed, and more than 70 people badly injured, several of whom died later from their injuries. It was the worse tube-train crash London Underground had ever experienced. The driver of the train was in good health, with no sign of alcohol or drugs in his blood. It was very unlikely that he had committed suicide. He had been a very conscientious driver whose record was clean since he had joined London Transport in 1969.

Train crews were worried by the Moorgate crash, because nothing was wrong with the train or the signalling equipment and track. So what did happen? Probably no one will ever know.

Quite a few passengers became concerned about the safety of tube-trains, and many asked questions about the crash. Others would peer into the driving cab to see the controls. All the train crews became more vigilant in their jobs, especially when arriving at terminus stations.

As a guard I certainly experienced some sticky moments. I once chased a male passenger, who must have been six times my size, down the platform. He had stolen a wallet from another passenger on my train, and as luck would have it I managed to persuade this huge mugger to return it. I handed the wallet back to my passenger and was able to continue the journey.

There were many other incidents involving passengers: sudden illness on the train, fighting, vandalism, mugging, security alerts and passengers wanting to board the train via the guard's gangway. With a mixed race of 'all sorts' to make up the world, you had to accept that some kind of incident would take place almost every day.

Many passengers would ask questions that I could not answer, ranging from taxi fares, times of buses and cinema opening times to queries concerning places of interest in London. Being a young lad from Essex, I had very little knowledge of the capital; everything was new to me as I had hardly ever been sightseeing. I found it very hard to digest the underground map with so many changes involved. Often I used to send passengers in the wrong direction, not realising my error until it was too late.

Although there were 32 train doors to choose from, many passengers used to argue with me when I refused them entry through my guard's door, and once I got punched in the stomach. Some passengers used to panic about getting on board the train; as it departed from the station the guard would look at least half way down the platform before closing his or her door, and this attracted some passengers to try and jump on while the train was moving. Many times I had to pull down the emergency handle to stop someone from being killed or injured.

One summer evening when I finished work, two strong, muscular men approached me outside Loughton station. They called me over to speak to them and naturally I thought they wanted directions. Suddenly I was punched in the face, knocking me to the ground. The police were alerted, but unfortunately they got away. The ambulance took me to hospital as I had a cut lip and was suffering from shock. Returning to work the following day, I discovered that the punch had been meant for another guard, and the two men had mistaken me for him. I was very angry indeed. However, I never received an apology as the matter was closed quickly without getting other staff in trouble.

Standing in the guard's gangway you were

The guard's gangway on the 1962 tube stock. The control panels are replicated on both sides so that the doors can be opened on either side of the train, and a bar can be swung up between the upright supports to keep out passengers, although many would try and board through the guard's door.

an easy target for abuse, or even physical violence. I lost count of how many times passengers swore at me about operating problems over which I had no control. We were taught never to argue back because this didn't solve anything. If you thought the passenger was going to give you a good hiding, you were told to run to a safe place and alert the police or another member of staff.

My most enjoyable times at work were working on the Epping to Ongar branch line, which was heaven compared to the rest of the Central Line. This 13-minute journey took you through the Essex countryside, and the first stop after leaving Epping was North Weald, a pleasant station with two small platforms and signal box. North Weald was a crossover point on the single-track line, allowing two shuttle trains running at the same time to pass one another.

Blake Hall station was next, the smallest and quietest on the entire underground system. With hardly any passengers to deal with, the Station Foreman, who lived in the station house, used to make traction engines for local shows. This station was eventually closed to save London Underground money, the whole line being under threat of closure.

Ongar, the terminus, had only one platform and an old, disused signal box that had been used until Epping signal cabin was able operate the station starter signal. There were no longer any points and crossovers, and the goods yard, with its old sheds and track that had been used in the steam age, was to stand there to decay for many years.

This branch line certainly had many memories, never to be forgotten. For example, scorpions were once found on the platform at Ongar. This certainly attracted the BBC and the local press, who wanted to view this

Arriving at North Weald on the sleepy Epping-Ongar branch. There used to be a passing loop here when two trains were run during peak hours.

All that remained of Ongar station, showing the disused signal box that was later dismantled by a railway society and rebuilt elsewhere.

unusual phenomenon for themselves. Little did anyone know that it was only a publicity stunt!

North Weald station also hit the headlines in the local press: 'Train driver bitten by rabbit'. Who could ever believe that a rabbit would jump through the cab window to bite the train driver? But maybe it did...

One morning, as the rain came down, the running rails between North Weald and Epping became slippery, and a train slid past the red home signal and through Epping's platform, crashing into the sand drag and knocking down the red stoplight before finally derailing itself. There was only one casualty, a pregnant woman who suffered shock.

As already mentioned, working as a guard you had to observe the platform from your gangway while the train was departing from a station. This was done for the safety of passengers, just in case someone became trapped in the doors and was dragged down the platform. One guard became distracted and hit his head on the platform headwall, resulting in his instant death.

There are more humorous and tragic stories about the underground throughout its history than you could ever imagine. Thousands of passengers have jumped under trains to take their own lives, while others have got their clothes or bags caught in the train doors and been dragged down the platform to a horrific death. There have been murders, rapes, muggings, assaults on staff and many other things that would send a cold shiver down your spine.

In July 1977 my wife gave birth once again, and we now had a son to complete the family. The cost of living was rising and my salary was very low, so we were finding it difficult to survive. Many guards on the underground were resigning from their jobs, as everyone else had the same problems. I applied for one vacant job as a salesman selling soft drinks, but I didn't get it as I had no experience; I also tried for other jobs, but without success.

London Transport was now suffering from a critical shortage of guards, so I stopped searching for employment elsewhere as this shortage gave me the chance of plenty of overtime, and I was able to pay my mortgage and other household bills once again without getting into debt.

The unions called for strike action to get higher salaries for London Transport staff of all grades, and London Transport had to give in because of the guard shortage, which was resulting in many train cancellations and overcrowding at stations. All staff received a decent pay rise, which also attracted more new recruits and eventually all the underground lines were fully staffed once again.

I was enjoying my job but I nonetheless often thought about promotion to train driver, both out of interest and to get a higher salary. Ten years of being a guard should have given me all the experience I needed, and every month all guards were given a driving trip, with the driver present, just to keep their hand in. I had plenty of practices over the years, so all I needed was to learn train equipment thoroughly – much more thoroughly than I had on my guard's course.

4
RULES AND REGULATIONS

I had now put in my application to train as a driver, but as train drivers were not needed at that time, I was going to have to wait for at least another year. However, once again this gave me plenty of time to study from books and hand-outs and to ask drivers questions about train equipment.

While I was waiting to attend the training school, hoping that this was going to be my last year as a guard, my driver and I went through an incident I have never forgotten. Honestly, it was the worse day of my life on the underground. Rowdy football supporters had boarded our train in their hundreds, and only a few hundred yards out of the station the passenger emergency handles were pulled, bringing the train to a stop. Luckily the police were nearby, but the interior of the train was vandalised and completely wrecked. Two passengers were stabbed and others were in a state of panic as fights broke out all over the train. After our hellish ordeal and once we had given our statements to the police, my driver and I were sent home suffering from shock.

During the ten years I worked as a guard, never once did I have the experience of a passenger jumping under my train. I would never have wanted this to happen in the first place, because it was something I'd always dreaded. It's bad enough for the driver to experience such a dreadful incident, and it takes a long time off work to get over the shock. My neighbour, whom I knew very well, jumped under a train on the Central Line. She was suffering from depression because her mother had died a few months before. It certainly must take a lot of courage to do this, because death is not guaranteed; survival is possible, even if you lose your limbs.

There are many horror stories on the underground, some of which would make your hair curl, like the one about the young couple who were playing a daring game. As a train arrived at the station, the young man pushed his girlfriend to frighten her. As she was falling on to the track he managed to catch her hands to save her. But it was too late – the train sliced her in half, with the young man still holding her hands.

As mentioned in the last chapter, many passengers have been dragged to their deaths as a result of their clothing or bags becoming caught in the doors. This happened to a Stationmaster on the Central Line. As he closed the middle cab door of the train he caught his overcoat in it. He was unable to open the door again and died a horrific death. Even passengers waiting innocently on the platform have been pushed under trains when the station has been overcrowded. Passengers have been known to walk down the tunnels, confronting a terrible death, while others have jumped from bridges and embankments, dying instantly. Many teenagers daring to cross the track have been electrocuted or badly burned.

Track maintenance staff have also been hit by trains or electrocuted. Although London Transport has always maintained a safety policy for its staff and passengers, safety rules are broken either deliberately or through carelessness. In any event, no safety rules could ever cover suicides or attempted suicides – anyone can break a safety rule if they feel they need to.

Admittedly, I and other staff have broken safety rules in the past, doing things like crossing the railway line and not using the official walkways in depots. But after you experience incidents you realise the dangers. You're risking your own life. It only takes one foot to slip on the ballast or on a slippery running rail, even though staff are trained to cross the track in all weather conditions; sometimes you have to in order to deal with incidents on the track.

Since the 1970s we have had many security alerts on the underground, and we never ignore any situation, whether in stations or on trains. Bombs have exploded on railway property a number of times, causing extensive damage. With over two million passengers every day using the underground, no one can afford to take chances, even when passengers innocently leave shopping bags or briefcases behind. While there remains the risk of a bombing campaign, all staff remain vigilant.

In my last few months of being a guard, I encountered armed police due to a misunderstanding between my driver and myself. A bank robber was being chased by police and they thought he had boarded our train. My driver asked me about him through the communication system on the train and I replied, 'I think he's gone.' My driver thought that I'd said, 'He has a gun'! As a result of our misunderstanding it became like a scene from a gangster movie as armed police rushed on to the platform.

The communication system between driver and guard on the 1962 stock was sometimes very unreliable, and tunnel dust used to block up the speakers. Trains were taken out of service as a result because this communication was vital, especially during emergencies. Normally the communication system would be tested before the train entered service. The guard and driver also had to carry out a brake test in the depot when preparing the train to leave, which involved calling to each other for instructions.

In preparation for the train to enter passenger service, the driver tested his 'dead man's handle' and checked the forward and reverse movement, train whistle, window wipers and auxiliary circuits. Meanwhile the guard would test his passenger doors and ensure that all the carriages where suitable for service. Every guard was also issued with a 'guards journal' in which to enter details of late running and any incidents; this was left on the train until it returned to the depot. These journals were abolished in the late 1970s because London Transport found other ways of recording information about trains in passenger service.

Many guards relied on their driver to get them out of trouble when there were defects on the train. The driver had more knowledge of train equipment, unless the guard had already passed his driver's examination and test and was just waiting for a vacant position in his depot. These were hard to come by, because many drivers were very content to stay where they were, although some did take promotion to become Station Inspectors. Vacant positions went on seniority in those days, giving the senior guards the first chance to fill any vacant positions.

Many drivers and guards were rostered together, which made life easy for everyone, because morale remained very high; train crews running together regularly knew how each other worked, and you certainly knew the difference when you were operating a train with a different driver or guard. Some drivers were faster, and some would brake harder than others, while unfamiliar guards were either too slow or too quick operating the doors in stations.

My first driver was a pirate radio fan, with radio stickers all over his old van. My second used to make metal boxes to carry his equipment. I used to call him Biffo, because he liked reading comics. Most train crews had nicknames they had to accept. My nickname was 'Grabber', because I was working every Sunday for double-time. We weren't allowed to work our rest-days during the week – this was a very strict union rule with the NUR and ASLEF. Sunday working was classed separately from weekdays and Saturdays; if you didn't want to work on Sunday, you had to put in for special leave, and there would be many volunteers to work your shift. Often I worked at other depots on Sundays; as we were also paid for travelling time, that was well worth doing.

'Sleet' training came once a year for drivers and guards. Our 'sleet train' had been converted in 1927, which gives you an idea of how the old trains had been built to last. The training consisted of the use of de-icing fluid and sleet brushes. To be honest, I hated this sleet train because it was a monster and prone to breaking down. It had no electric brake like our 1962 stock trains, so every driver had to brake using only the Westinghouse air brake, and if your technique was poor you had problems stopping. This was proved once when the sleet train crashed into the stops at Ongar. Before braking you had to ensure that you had enough train-line air stored in the auxiliary tanks, otherwise you would not stop.

Annual refresher courses not only catered for the monster sleet train – all train crews had their refreshers on 1962 stock. It was amazing how much knowledge you could forget in the course of a year. Some defects were very rare and the cure easily forgotten because you never had to deal with them in reality.

Regardless of what grade you were, you had to know the rules and regulations. Rules regarding the passing of red signals at danger were a top priority for drivers and guards. Semi-automatic signals were treated differently from automatic signals: semi-automatic signals were used in areas where points were located, while automatic signals were sited in other areas where the rules allowed a driver to pass them on a 'stop and proceed' basis without authority from the signalman, moving forward cautiously until the next signal was reached. When passing danger signals you had to take extra care to abide by the rule. Some drivers in the past crashed their trains into the one in front, often resulting in death or injury, which could happen if the driver forgot this important rule.

I was beginning to feel confident in my studies as I grew to understand everything

'Sleet' locomotives standing proudly outside Hainault depot. Their livery was changed from red to yellow, as seen here, in the 1970s. *R. Millhouse*

A typical automatic signal. These are located on sections of track where there are no points leading to depots and sidings, or crossovers. These signals are operated by the train itself occupying each section of track.

more clearly. Working as a guard I had more time to study while performing my duties in between stations. Each day I picked a subject concerning my studies and wouldn't give in until I understood every detail of it. As I have already said, to understand a subject, rather than learning it parrot fashion, you had to keep on asking yourself the magic word 'Why?'. *Why* does the flow of air run through the rotary valve into the brake pipe, and so on. This method of learning worked wonders providing that you remembered and didn't get it confused with another, similar subject.

At home, our two children needed their own bedrooms now they were out of the baby stage, so my wife and I decided to move to Epping, where we bought a three-bedroom semi-detached house near my parents' home. This move came at a good time because my promotion was getting nearer. At least while I was decorating and making the garden look suitable, I was still studying hard to achieve my boyhood ambition of becoming a train driver.

My original shyness had improved since I joined London Transport. I was getting used to dealing with people, chasing muggers, telling off passengers, and general crowd control. One of my friends, who was a Station Foreman, suggested that I should join the police force as a Special Constable like himself. At the time I was all for it as it sounded exciting – taking the law into my own hands! I applied for an interview to see the Chief Inspector and to my amazement he accepted me. However, before going to court to get sworn in I backed out; with late shifts I hardly saw my wife and children as it was, without spending my rest days walking the beat.

With money still a bit tight, I had a brainwave – I would make model rabbits, gnomes and cats out of cement. Unfortunately this became a complete disaster and a waste of time and money. My next idea involved making rocking-chairs from pegs. I sold hundreds of these by popular demand until I got fed up making them; our home had become a mini-factory, smelling of wood glue and varnish. Next came the copper pictures. I would spend hours on each one, etching out the copper. I'd always had some sort of hobby, but finally I decided to stick with gardening – at least my wife felt more contented with me, because before she never knew what I would be getting up to next!

At last London Transport decided to change the uniform. All operating staff were issued with a grey suit with a blue shirt. The Harold Wilson raincoat made you feel like a member of the Labour party, especially if you smoked a pipe, but the new uniform was OK until the tunnel dust began to make it look very dirty. Cleaning tokens were issued because the uniform needed to be cleaned on a regular basis – the old black uniform never showed the dust and grime from the tunnels.

Wearing the uniform has always been a strict rule. There was no excuse at all to wear your own clothes, because everyone received their issue every year – often your wardrobe was stacked with uniforms. London Transport was very generous with its supplies, ensuring that you never needed any more for at least another year.

In my last few months of being a guard, I was almost put off from becoming a train driver when a Central Line driver was killed applying the 'stop and proceed' rule at a red signal; he made the error of not going slowly once he had passed the signal, and crashed into the train in front, causing excessive damage. A few passengers were treated for shock in both trains, closing part of the Central Line for the rest of the day. Soon afterwards a train crashed into another in a tunnel, causing excessive damage to both.

With ten years experience as a guard behind me, I was now determined to take that long-awaited promotion. I still felt a bit nervous thinking of that day soon when I would be driving a tube-train, travelling through the dark dusty tunnels with my guard in the rear carriage on his gangway. My guard would then have to rely on me to deal with train defects and other operating problems. If I'd had more confidence in myself, I would have worried a little less – I was always thinking that the worst would happen, that I would be dismissed or demoted back to being a guard or even a railman. I hated my silly thoughts, flowing through my mind like a bad dream.

In the 1970s the terrorist bombing campaign had begun to sweep the principal English cities, and all Underground staff were briefed on what to look for concerning security alerts. I must admit that life began to get scary at work round this time, because the underground was a very easy target to hide bombs, especially in litterbins. Once London Underground experienced a nail bomb exploding at Oxford Circus, injuring some members of staff, which made everyone become very vigilant. On the District Line a train driver was involved in a security alert on the trackside, resulting in him being shot dead. This began to cause more concern for staff safety as well as that of the passengers.

One late afternoon, just as the rush hour had started, a passenger pulled down the emergency handle causing the train to stop at Chancery Lane station. Concerned, my driver and I went to the carriage only to find a brown briefcase on one of the passenger seats. We told all our passengers to leave the train and stand at the end of the platform until the police arrived. This briefcase looked very suspicious indeed, and we were expecting it to explode at any minute.

When the police finally arrived, they didn't want to open the briefcase, because they also thought it was very suspicious. Now the platform was clear because all the passengers had been told to wait upstairs in the booking hall. My driver and I remained on the platform out of sight, just in case there was going to be an explosion, and as the tension mounted my driver was asked to switch off all the train compressors to stop any vibrations that might trigger the bomb. Finally, one policeman summoned up all his courage and, saying his prayers at the same time, decided to open the briefcase at his own risk. While we were waiting for an explosion, he shouted out,

'False alarm!' This incident was one of many throughout the following years.

Having failed my car driving test twice a few years before, I decided to give it another try with a different driving school. My new driving instructor was much better than the previous ones, apart from the fact that he chain-smoked all the time. Perhaps my driving made him nervous! Actually, it wasn't too bad, apart from my reversing and three-point turns.

After six months I thought I was ready to pass the test, until I met my driving examiner. He looked old and very fed up with his life, judging by the expression on his face. He made me feel very nervous even before we got into the car for me to show him that I could drive just as well as anyone else on the road. The test began in the test centre car park, beside a busy main road. I started the engine and looked in the mirror, but the car wouldn't move forward – until the examiner reminded me to release the handbrake. As you can imagine, the test that followed was a disastrous experience and resulted in another fail certificate.

At this time I was riding a small motorcycle, having passed my motorcycle test first time without any trouble, so at last I could still get around. You hear of people passing their driving test after 50 attempts, and it makes you wonder if you are going to be one of them yourself! Before my next test I was told by one of my work colleagues to wear my railway uniform, as this would show the examiner that I had a responsible job. When my next test duly arrived I swallowed a few nerve pills my instructor had given me, and dressed in my railway uniform, trying to look as smart as possible. This time my examiner was a much younger man who even smiled at me. This made me feel more relaxed as I drove out of the car park – releasing the handbrake this time.

The driving test went very well, in fact better than I had expected, probably because I felt more relaxed this time. Suddenly the driving examiner said, 'Do you drive trains?' I told him I did. Actually I was still a guard, but I wasn't going to tell him that – anyway, I did drive trains once a month on my driving days. Arriving back at the test centre we sat in the car talking about railways for a few minutes until he handed me my pass certificate.

5
A DRIVER AT LAST

At long last the waiting was over and my opportunity for promotion arrived. I was still feeling very nervous, however, because I knew that it was going to be very tough. However, I was going to do my best, with as much confidence and determination as I could muster. Not only would I be letting myself down if I failed, I would also be letting down my wife and colleagues. After all, with my previous learning ability and experience of work, I had a better chance of succeeding than the other students.

Week one was rules and regulations, consisting of learning how signals work, which I knew anyway. We covered how to apply the rule about passing a red danger signal, wrong direction movements, single-line working, turning traction off in an emergency, and many other subjects. By the end of the week I felt completely exhausted and had a constant headache. At least I had the weekend off to recuperate by spending time with my wife and children, which was some consolation.

The weekend passed very quickly and it was soon time to face my worst week at the training school. Train equipment was the subject, and our first lesson consisted of learning about the two kinds of brake that we applied on the train. One was the Westinghouse air brake, the other an electric brake. Each brake had five different positions, and we had to learn each position, from the valves, pistons and electrical wiring to the train-line and main-line air supplies. Using electrical diagrams for the compressors, we learned how to isolate them in case of a main-line burst. The lesson also covered overcharging and undercharging, and the compressor isolation switches under the passenger seats; overcharging compressors could cause them to overheat and catch light.

Each train carried many fuses ranging from 40 amps to 10 amps, and these were situated behind the driver in the cab. Often these fuses were very hard to change, because they slotted into two electrical contacts; you had to be so careful when pulling them out in case you got an electric shock. Some drivers used to carry a gadget with which to pull them out. These fuses were about 6 inches long, the thickness depending on their amperage. We also had to learn about auxiliary wiring circuits; it was vital that we understood these, because of electrical defects.

Electricity and air operated everything on the tube-train. Main-line air was used to open the doors and operate the train whistle, electric brake and motors, while train-line air was used to operate the Westinghouse brake, passenger emergency handles, coupling engines, 'dead man's handle' and front and rear trip cocks.

The front trip was under the front of the train on the right-hand side. When a signal was at danger, the train stop belonging to that signal remained in an upright position, so if a train went past at danger the trip would hit the train stop, triggering the emergency brakes. This safety procedure couldn't fail unless the driver cut out the trip cock, which was very unlikely unless the cock failed. However, if it did fail, other safety procedures came into operation to stop the train from travelling too fast.

The train-line and main-line sometimes burst, due to a failure in the air pipes or hoses. If this happened the driver had to isolate certain cocks either outside the driving cab, or from the middle driving cabs, so as to regain forward movement. With an eight-carriage train, you had to treat defects as belonging to two trains, because of the two driving cabs in the middle. If one half of the train was defective, then you could still move forward, provided you had isolated the units. If you couldn't obtain forward movement at all, another train would come and push you from behind. If the couplings were not in their correct sequence, an emergency coupling adapter had to be used.

Defects were easy to learn about providing you understood the correct sequence of actions for each. If no forward movement was possible, first you would set your auxiliary overloads, then check that your train-line and main-line air was at the correct pressure, shown on a gauge in the driver's cab. Then you would try to move in reverse, ensuring that the 30 amp fuse was OK, and so on until you found the problem.

We also had to learn about the emergency equipment on and off the train. On the train were the detrainment steps, which were placed from the front coupler, allowing passengers to step down on to the track. Short-circuiting devices were placed on the positive and negative current rails, stopping any electric current going past them, while detonators were placed on the running rails to warn other drivers of the danger ahead; these detonators would explode if a train ran over them. Underneath the passenger seat was a bag of sand, used for small fires on the train or track. There were also ice scrapers, in case the conductor shoes didn't pick up the electricity from the current rails.

Before my oral examination, I was sent back to my home depot for more training. As part of this I had to drive a train in passenger service with a driver instructor. I did make a few errors, such as dropping the 'dead man's handle', causing the train to apply its emergency brake; I also overran a few stations because I wasn't quick enough in applying the brake. I found it a nerve-racking experience at first, mainly because I knew that one day I would be driving on my own.

After three days of this I went back to the training school for my oral examination. All the other students were to be examined that same day. Students always sat in pairs with their instructor, and I and my companion were chosen to take our examination last. The stern-looking examiner couldn't find an empty classroom because every room was occupied, and finally we settled for the stage in the large hall used for social functions. It was certainly very strange sitting there with the long blue stage curtains around us. I felt very nervous, as my chain-smoking demonstrated. Once everyone was comfortable, it was time to begin.

The examiner looked at me first. 'Pretend I have come from abroad, wanting to know all about your trains,' he said. I started to explain the many compressors and motors they had, until I got confused when it came to talking about the defects. I was getting very annoyed with myself, because I was so nervous, so he gave me time to recover and light up another cigarette while the other student answered a few questions. He wasn't doing very well, which made me feel cleverer, if only because he seemed to be getting the tough questions.

After the tea break it was time to face that stern-looking examiner again. The other student faced his implacable interrogation until he failed. I thought that my chances of passing this examination were going to be the same and wished some other examiner at the school was sitting there instead of him. However, my nerves began to settle as I answered the questions correctly, although I still made a few errors – as could only be expected under those conditions. Suddenly the examiner banged his fist hard on the table – everything shook, including me! – all because I had got my sequence wrong in explaining the flow of air in the braking position.

After seven long hours of answering questions, I was beginning to feel exhausted. My examiner must have started feeling the same way, because he stopped banging his fist on the table. He told me that I had passed, but that I must ensure that I understood the subjects about which I had got confused by reading them up again. Nonetheless I was able to tell my wife and work colleagues that I had passed my oral examination. But there was more to come before I became a fully qualified train driver. I had to spend one week with another train driver to brush up on my driving technique, then three days of stock training, refreshing my memory of train defects and equipment. This was vital to ensure that you knew your job thoroughly before you were let loose on your own.

The final stage was the road test, when a Divisional Manager sat with you in the driver's cab, observing your driving and braking. This was followed by lots of questions concerning train equipment and rules and regulations. Once this task was over, you finally became a qualified train driver.

Before I could drive a train in passenger service, I had to do my 'hiking'. This consisted of walking around all the depots and sidings on the Central Line. Every driver had to do this, because it was very important for stabling to know where the different roads and shed roads were. You had to know every shunting or colour-light signal for entering or leaving the depots. You also learned how to take the train through the train wash and how to pull out the shed leads. These leads plugged into the receptacle box on the side of the train and provided 650 volts to the train when it was stabled on shed roads that didn't have any current rails. If the train was stabled in the shed roads, the train crew would prepare it for service, providing that the first carriage was on the current rails outside the shed. It was the guard's job to pull out the shed leads and hang them on a hook swinging above; often this would take quite a few attempts, as the leads were heavy. Sidings were very straightforward to learn about, providing you knew where to stop without hitting the buffers or stoplight. The outlet end of every siding ended with a shunt signal before the main line began.

At last the day had arrived when I would have to test my nerves and ability by driving a passenger train in service on my own, something almost every driver dreaded. If problems were to occur, it would be up to me to sort them out, although at least the guard was there to assist if I needed advice. I felt very nervous, thinking of all the worst things that could happen.

As my guard closed the train doors at the station, he gave me the bell to signal that they were all closed, I was now ready to drive my train to the next station and so on until my duty finished. Admittedly, I did overrun one station by two carriages, because my Westinghouse braking wasn't up to scratch; I needed more practise because the pure air brake was a matter of trial and error, as opposed to the easily controlled electric brake. I was pleased to get that first day finished, the day when I realised what a huge responsibility it was to drive a train. Every driver used to write their defects in a notebook for future reference, just in case they forgot the vital knowledge they had been taught.

My wife was very pleased that I had succeeded in becoming a train driver, knowing that I had wanted this promotion for a very long time. Now that I was earning a better salary at least I could spend more time at home with my family, without having to work every Sunday like I used to.

My promotion didn't mean that I would be driving trains straight away. Often I had to carry out guard's duties until a vacant driver's position became available. However, with my long service I was always first in line if any driver went sick from work. Within a few months I became rostered permanently when another driver took retirement.

A few weeks later I had to do night duty for a week. I used to enjoy working nights for the peace and quite. We had four hours' rest just sitting in the depot until the train was ready to enter service at about 5am, after you and your guard had prepared it. Sometimes if the temperature was warm in the depot we would sit on the train, because the rest room used to get quite busy with other train crews and depot staff.

One particular morning when I was arriving at White City station from the depot, I heard a very strange sound above me, a very low-pitched whirling noise, reminding me of the spinning tops I used to play with as a child. To my amazement, when I looked up I saw a huge circular dullish white object moving very

My first week as a qualified train driver, in July 1981, at Loughton Sidings. My boyhood ambition had come true at last.

slowly at a low altitude. I called my guard over the train radio to witness this unusual sight, and after two minutes this strange object suddenly sped off at great speed towards the stars, leaving us dumbfounded.

When we got back to the depot and told everyone what we had seen it didn't go down very well. No one believed us – they thought we were dreaming or winding them up. But depot staff at Acton Works and a train driver on the District Line had seen the flying object that same morning. That was the third sighting I had of unidentified flying objects on the railway. I believe they do exist, because there must be life somewhere else in the universe.

6
NORTHERN EXPOSURE

My job as a train driver on the Central line has been an interesting one, and I have always been fascinated with the history of the underground system, especially the Central Line. The original 'Central London Railway' of 1900 ran from Wood Lane in the west to the steeply curved Bank station in the City. Extending the line to Liverpool Street in 1912 caused problems because of the Bank of England underground vaults, which is the reason why there are so many sharp bends.

In the days of steam the eastern end of the line was part of the Great Eastern Railway, running from Ongar to Liverpool Street via Leyton. London Transport extended the Central Line by tunnelling from Leyton to Liverpool Street, and this section opened in 1947. By 1949 electric tube-trains were running from Epping to West Ruislip and Ealing Broadway, although the Epping to Ongar branch continued to run steam trains until electrification was introduced in November 1957. Without steam trains to carry coal to the good yards, the latter were discontinued and were eventually transformed into car parks. Because of the electrification and the frequency of the train service all the level crossings were removed apart from that at North Weald, and the local councils had to build road bridges over the railway to cater for the road traffic. Also more footbridges and high wire fences were erected to stop people crossing the electrified track on the level.

Only two stations on the Central Line have ever been closed: British Museum, between Tottenham Court Road and Holborn, in 1933, and Wood Lane, situated east of White City, in 1947. Other changes saw Loughton station moved further east, and Chigwell Lane station renamed Debden in 1949.

I was now beginning to feel more settled driving trains, having coped successfully with many train defects and other operating problems. As when I was a guard, my favourite part of the Central Line was the Epping to Ongar branch; this pleasant 13-minute journey through the Essex countryside certainly suited me. Many other drivers would change their shifts with me so I could happily enjoy my driving without going through those dark dusty tunnels.

My favourite Central Line stock was that of 1962, because it was very reliable and very comfortable for our passengers. The driver's cab wasn't so comfortable for the driver, however, as it was small and had a hard seat. The cab doors were very low so you would often hit your head when leaving the cab. Some modifications were made, such as the installation of a public address system and train radio, while de-icing equipment and sleet brushes were also fitted on some trains.

The months passed quickly, and I was given a nomination form – against my wishes – to change to another line. Every driver on the Central Line had to travel on another line until a vacant position occurred back on the Central, and normally they were sent to the Bakerloo or Northern Lines, which were less popular. I asked to be sent to the Northern Line at High Barnet because it was easiest to get to, travelling by car. My first day I nearly caused a riot when a Northern Line guard who had passed his driver's examination started arguing with me. Before I arrived he had been covering a vacant driver's position and he felt

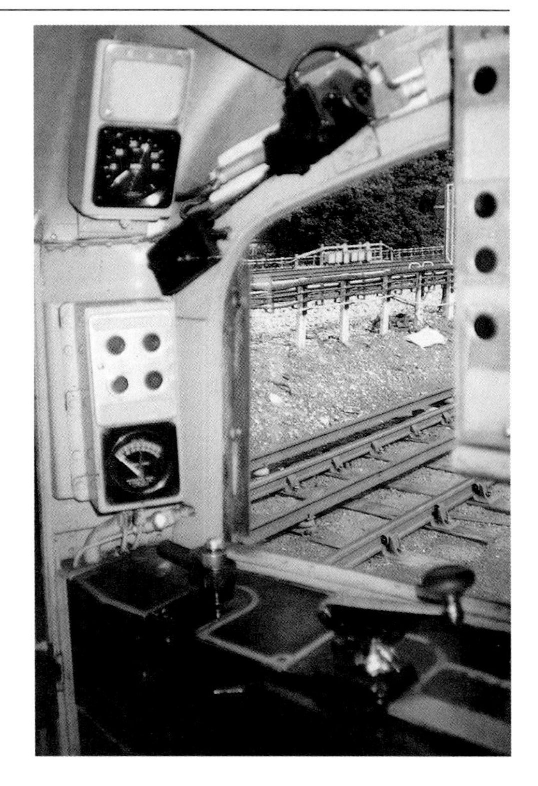

The 1962 Central Line stock was my favourite, although the driver's cab, seen here, was not the most comfortable.

it wasn't fair that I had taken over, because he was going to lose a lot of money by going back to working as a guard. I told him I hadn't wanted the job in the first place.

The Northern Line was certainly different from the Central Line in every way imaginable. Only the rules and regulations were the same, because these applied to all underground lines on the network. I spent two days learning about the train equipment of the 1972 stock in Golders Green depot. Road training with another driver followed, until I understood the line. My training only took three weeks because I had already had training on the 1962 stock on the Central Line. The Northern Line also ran 1959 tube stock, but this was similar to the 1962 stock.

Once I had completed my entire training and road test, I still didn't feel contented – in

Withdrawn former Northern Line tube stock, from 1959, in Ruislip Depot.

Withdrawn former Northern Line 1972 tube stock. I had to learn to drive both the 1959 and 1972 stock during my time on the Northern Line; luckily the 1959 stock was similar to the Central Line 1962 stock.

fact I felt very uncomfortable. I hated every day and longed to return to the Central Line. Travelling by car to and from work used to take over an hour each way through the busy streets, and if I had chosen to travel by train the journey would have taken even longer. However, I managed to survive five weeks until a vacant position became available on the Central Line, due to a driver taking promotion to work on the stations as an Inspector.

When I returned to the Central Line it was not to my own depot at Loughton, but to Hainault, although I didn't mind because at least I was back where I wanted to be. I was now driving trains on a roster, which meant that I could plan my social life much better and spend more time with my family.

Six months later a train driver from Loughton depot took promotion and I was sent back there to fill his vacant position. It was nice to be back with my old work colleagues once again.

That same year I was sent into hospital to have an operation for a trapped nerve in my leg, which had caused a numb thigh and back problems. After my operation I could hardly walk, being in so much pain from the stitches. After a few weeks this pain began to ease and I returned to my duties, perhaps a bit too soon – however, as my job didn't involve heavy manual work I had nothing to worry about, providing I took things easy until I was completely recovered.

When I arrived back at my depot from my sick leave, I carried on straight away with my driving duties. The service was running as normal without any delays and I was quite content to drive my train westbound on my second trip, until I got held at the home signal at Bank station. The train in front had broken down due to a burst train-line on the front unit. From where I was waiting I could see the defective train in the platform at Bank with the train crew and station staff walking up and down the platform. After 10 minutes the passengers alighted from the defective train, which then left the station at normal speed.

When I arrived at the station I was confronted with a packed platform full of passengers. When we finally left we had a clear run up to the home signal at Bond Street, then we were held again at a traction current indicator, which showed that the traction current ahead had been switched off.

To my amazement I found that the defective train in front had crashed into another train at Marble Arch. The train crew hadn't isolated the train in the correct way, so they had no brakes with which to avoid this catastrophic crash. Luckily no one was killed or injured as both train crews ran through the carriages, knowing what was going to take place.

I couldn't reverse my train to Oxford Circus because another train was standing there, and other trains were held back right down to Holborn. Consequently my guard and I set up the emergency ladder on the front coupler, and finally led our passengers through the dark and dusty tunnel to Bond Street station.

Five hours later the Line Controller decided that every driver being held from Holborn to Bond Street was to drive his train under the wrong direction movement rule back to Holborn station, where they could use the siding to return to their eastbound journey. This process seemed to take ages, because when moving in the wrong direction you had no colour light signals and had no idea how far away the train in front was.

Apart from suffering from a splitting headache and sweating from the heat and dust in the tunnel, the stitches in my leg had split open after walking down the emergency ladder so many times. I was very pleased to get home, even if it was five hours late. I didn't go back to work the following day because my stitches needed hospital treatment.

After a year driving trains I had become more experienced. I had now encountered many operating problems, giving me more confidence in my job and myself. Many people don't realise the responsibility train drivers have, especially in emergency situations. We all try to do our best with the knowledge gained from our regular training and to ensure that we put safety first at all times for our passengers and other staff.

My twin brother resigned from London Transport to become a chauffeur for Shakin' Stevens when he starred in a West End musical. He would often give us free theatre tickets, and such evenings out didn't cost us anything at all, because travelling was free on the underground for my wife and I with our free travel passes. My brother had enjoyed his working life on the underground, and once the bright lights of showbiz started to dim, he began to regret his resignation. Over the years I have seen many staff regretting such a move and being unable to return, and other staff who have retired with great sadness. Once the railway gets into your blood, it will always remain because you can never compare it with any other job.

Despite the regular safety training and practice on emergency procedures that train drivers received every year, many incidents happened that were beyond our control. During the 1980s one of our Central Line drivers was driving happily through the tunnel when suddenly his train hit a large road drill, which completely wrecked the driver's cab and he was very lucky to escape injury – the workmen above at street level hadn't realised the depth to which they were drilling! This incident could have been much worse if the drill had actually bored into one of the carriages instead, causing a major disaster.

Children have been known to throw heavy objects from footbridges, causing extensive damage to the trains and in some cases injuring the driver. London Transport had to put wire cages over all the footbridges to stop such vandalism, as well as preventing people from jumping to their deaths. It was possible to try to stop most incidents, but impossible to stop trespassers from gaining entry to railway property to cause damage. These people found ways to get through 6-foot barbed-wire fencing, or to gain entry unseen from a station. Outside security companies with CCTV cameras were hired to patrol station premises and depots to keep vandalism down to a minimum, which was important, as vandalism can cause injury or death.

One of the main safety issues for drivers was the question of stepping from the train on to the track, especially in tunnel sections. The rules stated that the train must be fully secured before a driver takes this action. Since the train was fitted with an electrical brake, this was actually unsafe because the brake fuse could blow, releasing the brakes and allowing the train to run over the driver. Some drivers applied the Westinghouse brake, as this could not fail. Other drivers went for maximum safety by applying their handbrakes.

Drivers were always told to secure their trains, and to take their control and position keys with them if they had to leave it. This was mainly for the benefit of passengers, because there was always a chance that a passenger might try to drive the train. This was proved once when a guard fainted on his gangway. One passenger decided he didn't want to be late for work as a result, and operated the doors until he reached his destination. The guard's condition was only discovered when the train doors didn't close after the passenger had departed, alerting the driver that something was wrong.

One passenger at Liverpool Street used to stand on the platform shouting 'All change!' when trains stopped in the platform. All the passengers used to leave the train, until staff told them it was a false alarm.

Being a train driver carries the same responsibilities as an airline pilot. It doesn't matter whether passengers are travelling 32,000 feet above the earth in the clouds or 100 feet underground. The pilot or driver is in charge of the safety of his or her passengers, and both are trained to deal with emergencies to prevent injury or death.

Reading the daily newspaper I found on a train one morning, I found an article concerning a man who had discovered a Roman treasure trove using a metal detector. This article remained on my mind all day, because my ambition was to become rich before I got too old to enjoy it. Within two weeks I had purchased a metal detector and set forth to find fame and fortune in the Essex countryside. My first step was to get permission from landowners to go on their land. To do this, I showed one landowner how I retrieved an item from the ground without causing any damage to the grass. He was impressed, but permission was not granted in the end, because his solicitor decided I might cause damage. Two years later a motorway was built across the land, causing more damage than anything I would have done!

One kind farmer gave me permission to search his fields, which I did until I got chased by a herd of cattle. I had never run so fast in all my life – it scared the life out of me. I decided not to revisit the farm after that experience. Anyway, up to that time I had only found hundreds of ring-pulls and general rubbish.

One day I received a telephone call from a lady who had lost her wedding ring on her vast front lawn and required my metal detector services to search for it. After two days, to my surprise my metal detector found it. The lady was so pleased that she gave me a big hug and a kiss on the cheek.

My next task was detecting in shallow rivers, again once I had got permission from the landowner. To my amazement I found an old Chinese bell buried beneath the pebbles in a river. I took it to the British Museum and discovered that it was about 100 years old, but only worth about £20 at the time.

When this hobby became popular, many people began to go on land without permission, causing damage by digging holes with garden spades instead of a small trowel. These people began to give metal detecting a bad name, making it harder to obtain permission from landowners.

My last task was scanning beaches, although again I only found hundreds of ring-pulls and the odd coin. My next-door neighbour used to keep me company, hoping that he would find his fame and fortune as well. However, after six months I decided to give up the hobby because it was so time-consuming.

7
TURMOIL AND TRANQUILLITY

My marriage was now in its 13th year and I was happy and contented with my family and job. I had everything to live for and wouldn't have changed my life for anything. My children were now at the infants school, which they enjoyed very much, learning something new each day. All through my marriage we had rarely had any upsets. We never argued as we were both the placid type and got on so well with one another. But suddenly our marriage began to take a turn for the worse. As we never argued I found it very hard to deal with our problems until it was too late. The result was a divorce.

This left me in a state of profound self-pity, my heart broken. Despite the sleepless nights I tried my hardest to carry on with my duties at work. Often I would have tears rolling down my face as I drove my train. I lost concentration at work because my mind was in a terrible muddle with so many other things to think about. I therefore began to take time off before I injured or killed someone. This went on for some months before I came to terms with the divorce. Unfortunately my time off work led me to the discipline board, where all I was told was to leave my problems at home. They didn't realise that it was totally impossible to sit in a driver's cab without thinking of your problems.

My heartbreak continued when my young brother was taken into hospital and sadly died. Now everyone in the family was heartbroken, especially my parents. Having to console my parents at the same time as coping with my divorce was the hardest thing I had ever had to do. It was impossible to carry on with my duties as I couldn't concentrate and I had become a danger to passengers and myself. London Transport accepted my sickness this time, and offered me help and counselling. This helped a lot until I was fit enough to return to work, which I did after my brother's funeral, although still not feeling 100 per cent. I had to accept that life had to go on and I had to put my job first no matter what turmoil my life was in.

After a few days I began to settle down in my driving duties and was gradually getting my concentration back until I arrived at Liverpool Street to face the most dreaded and horrid experience of a lifetime. As I approached the platform a male passenger suddenly jumped in front of my train. I applied the emergency brake and dropped the 'dead man's handle'. I felt totally numb. Some passengers were screaming while others stood there in amazement and shock. My radio 'mayday' call to the Line Controller failed because my radio decided to stop working at this crucial moment. Luckily, a member of staff was on the platform to raise the alarm.

The traction current was switched off, immediately stopping all the other passenger trains on the eastbound line. While my guard and I laid the short-circuiting devices at either end of the train, the station staff were coping with the disembarkation of passengers through one set of double doors, because only half the train was at the platform. When the emergency services arrived, they had to crawl underneath the train into the so-called 'suicide pit' to investigate the state of the body. This was a procedure to ascertain whether the person was dead or alive before anyone thought about moving the body.

The medics confirmed that he was dead, so I had to drive my train slowly over the body until the rear carriage was completely clear. Once the body was placed on a stretcher and taken away, sand was thrown into the blood-stained 'suicide pit' and the traction current was switched back on to return train services to normal, albeit running late.

I had to drive my train out of service to Leytonstone, then wait for the police so I could give them a statement on this terrible incident. Once the police was satisfied with my statement, my guard and I were sent home.

Still in a state of shock, I needed at least four to five weeks to recuperate. After that I had to face the coroner, something I had been dreading because I detested the formality of the courts. Officially I was on a manslaughter charge until it was proven that the male passenger had committed suicide.

With my nervous disposition in court, the judge told me off for not talking loudly enough. Indeed, my nerves got the best of me as I could hardly speak at all throughout the hearing, standing there in the witness box with many eyes peering at me. I was beginning to think that this court case was more nerve-racking than the actual suicide had been.

When my life began to return to normal, my work colleagues decided that I should take their advice and restart my social life. I spent many occasions at singles nightclubs hoping to meet the woman of my dreams, even though I was no hunk of a guy with only average looks. My courting days proved disastrous, with something going wrong with every lady I took out. One woman invited me to her home for dinner, but as soon as I entered her hallway I stepped on her foot and broke her toe. On another occasion I was driving a lady home from an expensive restaurant, and all was well until I suggested that she should 'come back to my place for coffee'. She looked at me in fury and demanded that I run her home. I didn't realise that the phrase had quite different connotations, being so out of date with modern courtship rituals. I never saw her again.

More disastrous meetings took place, only to end with me sitting indoors on my own looking at a blank wall, thinking of what to do next to conquer my loneliness. I had never enjoyed my own company at the best of times, and I wasn't in the frame of mind to get married again – I just wanted female company for friendship and fun.

In 1986 I met a married lady who was in the middle of her own divorce, although she and her husband were still living with one another. I had to tread very carefully, as I didn't want to get involved with the husband. We used to meet at a spiritualist church with my so-called girlfriend, who was actually an accomplice – her mother – giving my real girlfriend an excuse to meet me.

Once my girlfriend's divorce came through, her husband moved out, still unaware that she was seeing anyone, until one afternoon he knocked on the door while I was there. I quickly ran upstairs and hid in one of the bedrooms. To my amazement he walked into the bedroom as I was sitting on the bed. As I gulped in shock, he said 'Hello', then walked downstairs slamming the front door behind him. We never saw him again after that.

My girlfriend asked me to move in with her and her four daughters for a trail period, to see how we might all get on together before making it permanent. As I spent more time in her home than mine, I decided to move in while I was selling my home in Epping. Now I had found the woman of my dreams, I began to feel more contented in my life and to regain my confidence in my job. I was now free from any worries, giving me wonderful thoughts for the future.

One afternoon, while driving my train towards Leytonstone on a westbound run, I was held at the home signal for some time. To my amazement the Line Controller called on the train radio, asking me to ensure that all the passengers on my train sat in the first carriage with their heads ducked down away from the windows. Suddenly a police helicopter started hovering above my train, and armed police appeared on the railway track. They were looking for an armed bank robber, who was supposed to have run down the railway embankment on to the track.

My orders from the Line Controller were that my guard and I were to prepare for detrainment using the emergency ladder, and it was confirmed that the traction current had been switched off to allow this to take place as quickly as possible. I was to remain on the train for safety reasons, mainly to ensure that the train wouldn't roll away if the brakes accidentally released. I found this very exciting, being involved with the police, and was watching everything going on until an armed policeman told me to keep my head down. The police procedure seemed to take a very long time, until finally they caught their bank robber, but were unable to find his gun. This delayed the service even more as they searched the long grassy embankments. I was beginning to feel dehydrated, and my throat felt as though it was swelling up. When the police finished their duties, train services resumed once it was confirmed that traction current was switched on. I was relieved at Leytonstone by another driver so I could go and make a statement.

To my horror I was told I had to attend an incident inquiry at a later date, because my passengers had stepped over live current rails when we detrained them. This could have resulted in injury or death if a passenger had touched or slipped on to the 650-volt current rail. The national press, radio and television soon made this incident well known to the public the following day – 'Passengers walk on live track'. I was beginning to worry about my future employment with London Transport.

However, the railway enquiry board decided that I had carried out my duties correctly. I had confirmed that the traction current had been switched off in the section where my train stood. Other staff got the blame because I had no control over the section of track ahead. Even the national newspaper stated that it wasn't the driver's fault. It was very reassuring to read this before the enquiry took place.

I was now living in Woodford Green in Essex with my girlfriend and her four daughters. We decided to make a fresh start by moving home, to escape the memories for both of us, although her youngest daughters were not very keen to move because of their school. I managed to find a house to rent in Theydon Bois; in fact, it was the station house that belonged to London Transport. It was going to be ideal living on the station, as I would have no problems travelling to work by car like I used to.

With plenty of decorating to do, because the station house had been empty for three years, we soon made it comfortable to live in, although I had to hire a scaffolding stage to paint the high ceilings. With no central heating, we found the house freezing cold in the winter, but the lounge had a large open fireplace in which we burned old wooden logs I found on the railway embankments.

As my favourite hobby was gardening, I quickly cultivated the garden and entered it for the London Transport garden competition, since it was owned by London Transport and on display to passengers. I succeeded in receiving a First Class award for my efforts.

In the garden stood a very old brick-built shed, which I decided to tidy inside because it was in a complete mess. On a wooden shelf I found a newspaper dating back to 1951. The headline read 'Policeman shoots himself'. I gave this newspaper to the police at Epping, and they were amazed to learn the truth, as no one knew the correct story involving the reason why he had shot himself. This was published in the local paper and I felt very pleased with myself for discovering it.

On 18 November 1987 31 people died in the King's Cross fire. It broke out as commuters were heading home at around 7.30pm, when a passenger on an escalator lit a cigarette and dropped the match on to the wooden treads. The fire fed on the grease on the moving stairway and within 10 minutes it had engulfed the wooden steps. Fifteen minutes later the flames had reached the King's Cross ticket hall, then erupted in a fireball, filling the crowded station with poisonous black smoke. Many who died were killed instantly and many suffered terrible burns.

The Managing Director of London Underground Ltd, which had succeeded London Transport in 1985, said that there was no need for alarm, because all wooden escalators would be replaced with new ones

Above Theydon Bois station, showing the station house in the background where I was living at the time.

Below The garden at Theydon Bois, my pride and joy and an oasis of tranquillity after the turmoil of the preceding year. It won me a First Class award in the London Underground station garden competition.

constructed from non-combustible materials. Furthermore, all rooms would be fitted with smoke detectors. Staff throughout the underground system were given fire training to deal with fire and evacuation procedures.

While this extensive work was being carried out, London Underground employed extra staff because every room on a station had to be checked at least every hour, day and night, and it became compulsory to receive fire training every year.

London Underground also completely banned smoking on every station and train. Even staff weren't allowed to smoke in their canteens or rest rooms, especially in the tunnel sections. Any passenger caught smoking was first warned, and if the warning was ignored the police would make an arrest. Any staff caught smoking were dismissed instantly without any warning. Any reports of smouldering, no matter where, were always dealt with by the fire brigade. This attendance of the fire brigade at false alarms and any slight smouldering on the track was costing London Underground thousands of pounds each day, but no one was going to take any chances that more lives might be lost.

London's underground system has always maintained very high safety standards, no matter how far back into the past you look. When a disaster like the Moorgate crash or the fire at King's Cross happens, more safety rules are implemented. We can only learn from these disasters to improve safety all the time, no matter what era we live in.

One day I decided to take my girlfriend and her daughters to visit the London Transport Museum. I feared that the girls wouldn't take a lot of interest, but to my surprise they did. I was showing them how to drive a tube train on some old 1938 stock, when a museum attendant asked if I needed help. When I told him I already knew because I drove tube-trains, he looked quite shocked and walked away.

Every time I visit London I always take my camera with me, because it is a wonderful city, full of history and character. Sightseeing can be very interesting providing you don't mind standing in queues with the tourists, and the pigeons swooping around you after food.

8
ALL CHANGE

One year after the King's Cross fire I decided to get married, because we had come to the end of a three-year trial period living together. This trial period wasn't planned – it was just that it had taken me three years to finally kneel down and propose. As money was short my wife made her own dress and bridesmaids' gowns for her daughters. We had a church wedding, followed by a reception in a hall, sharing our happiness with family, friends and my railway colleagues. A short honeymoon followed, in a posh hotel in Dover.

Returning to work after my honeymoon it was back to normal, as I continued with my driving duties on the Central Line. My regular guard transferred to another depot and was replaced with another guard who was great to work with apart from the fact that he was very short-tempered. I had to be careful how I spoke to him, making sure that I asked him politely to do things concerning his duties and making tea. However, he did hit another driver on the head with a chair on one occasion and got into many arguments.

Our tube trains were very reliable and gave us very little trouble with defects. Only once did I experience my electric brake fuse blowing half-way down a platform. I quickly applied the emergency Westinghouse brake, slightly overrunning the station. Once I had changed the fuse we continued normally in passenger service. Admittedly this experience does shake you up at first, because when the brake fuse blows, a very loud audible warning goes off when you put the brake in the application position.

I experienced two fires on my train when the fire brigade had to be called in. The first time, the train resistors underneath the front carriage caught alight, and the heat was so intense that it caused the wooden floor to become very hot; fortunately these floors were treated so as not to catch fire, otherwise there could have been a terrible panic. My second fire incident was when my motors caught alight. This time the fire brigade had to crawl underneath the train to extinguish the fire. It was my responsibility to ensure the traction current had been switched off and to lay down the short-circuit devices at each end of the train before the firemen attempted to crawl underneath. One fireman said, 'I am relying on you, otherwise you can tell my wife the reason why I didn't come home.' Not only did I have to ensure that the traction current had been isolated, I also had to check that the train had its four handbrakes on to stop it from moving.

Besides incidents like this we did always manage to find time for some humour on the underground with staff and passengers. With passengers you had to tread very carefully, making sure you said the right thing at the right time without upsetting them. Humour on the trains and stations is very rare, because passengers hardly ever speak to each other unless they have to.

One driver decided to give his passengers a laugh that went terribly wrong. He pretended he was blind and walked along the platform with a white stick, asking passengers to show him to the driver's cab. The humorous driver was reported and lost his job.

Many drivers have been disciplined for speaking their minds on their train's public address system, especially when they have given London Underground a bad name and blamed them for incidents that were taking place. This practice is very dangerous because you never knew who is listening.

The signalman at Liverpool Street station used to stand on the westbound platform singing opera to the passengers. They used to enjoy this, because he was an excellent singer, and there were never any complaints from the millions of passengers who used the station.

One of our Central Line drivers used to make strange noises over the public address system on his train, sounding very similar to Eddie Murphy. The passengers were very impressed, and he ended up appearing on television.

Often passengers would ask how long the next train would be. Once I replied, 'The same length as this one.' This didn't make the passenger laugh as she thought I was being insulting.

Some humour from staff could be very dangerous, especially when you were sprayed with a bottle of perfume! This happened to me once, and resulted in an argument with my wife, because she could smell the perfume on my shirt collar as soon as I arrived home and thought I had been seeing someone else.

One afternoon I was preparing my train for service in the depot when suddenly I heard someone knock on my cab door. I opened the door wondering who was there and to my surprise found a passenger. He explained that he had fallen asleep on the train on his way to work and had found himself in the depot when he woke up. He had been hoping a member of staff would find him, having been sitting on the train for five hours in the depot. I reported this to the shunter before moving the train, and he didn't believe me at first until he got the depot manager to investigate.

The best prank on a Station Manager I ever encountered was the time one asked me for a memo stating why I was late booking on. He expected me to use one of the various excuses for lateness like oversleeping, heavy traffic or domestic problems. I decided to write something completely different, although I knew he wasn't going to believe me. I wrote out two memos, as I knew the first would end up in the rubbish bin. The first stated that two women in a lay-by had stopped me on my way to work and had got in my car and seduced me. It was worth it to see the manager's face when he read it. Of course, the memo did end up in the rubbish bin as I had predicted.

One early evening, when I had finished my duty at Leytonstone, I joined the passengers standing on the platform waiting for the Epping service. When the train eventually arrived I got on and sat down. After a few minutes I started talking to a young lady sitting opposite me, demonstrating how staff can be friendly without being insulting or even chatting someone up for a date. Two months later, to my amazement, I saw her again at my stepdaughter's wedding. She was my son-in-law's sister. To this day we talk about this strange coincidence.

Most of the humour on the underground happens in the staff restrooms and canteens. No matter what drivers get up to, there is always someone to make a joke out of it. Sometimes this can be upsetting, but you have to take it all in good part and laugh it off. It even happens when a driver gets injured, like the time one of our drivers walked into a support post on the platform while going to the rescue of another driver who was being assaulted by a passenger. This event caused endless humour with cartoon drawings of the injured driver being pinned on the notice board.

Perhaps we all sound like kids, and we are certainly young at heart, but the simple reason is that once we are driving our trains we have no reason for humour as we all take our jobs very seriously.

All humour came to a sudden stop when we heard that our depot at Loughton was to be closing down in the very near future. The whole Epping to Ongar branch line was under threat of closure, with many new changes proposed to take place over all the underground system, which would effect all grades of staff. The trade unions began to do battle with London Underground over the proposed changes, and this caused wildcat strikes among all staff, bringing London to a standstill on a regular basis for months. As these strikes began to worsen, London

Underground decided to send its top officials to visit every depot on the network. They tried to explain that the new changes would be beneficial for everyone: no more double-time Sunday work, as all duties throughout the week would pay the same, no extra salary when working late or night shifts, remote booking on and off at other depots, and getting rid of all the guards, as one-man-operated trains were being proposed. I for one couldn't see how I was going to benefit from these proposed plans. I also couldn't understand why they wanted to change everything as the underground was running a good service and morale was high.

As the wildcat strikes continued, London Underground converted two of its Craven stock tube-trains from Hainault to run on the Epping to Ongar branch line. This stock was painted red with only three carriages, and of course one-man-operation only. I enjoyed driving these trains on the branch. One of them was kept at Loughton sidings and the other at Hainault depot, and they used to swap over on alternative days for maintenance work when London Underground ran a rush-hour service only, instead of an all-day service as they had done for many years.

Despite the wildcat strikes London Underground gradually brought in the first stages of the changes throughout the entire underground system. Every member of staff taking strike action was sent a letter threatening instant dismissal unless they came back to work. Many staff began to return to their depots and stations, and others also followed suit, mainly the more militant ones. Once London Underground had succeeded in rounding up its entire striking staff, ASLEF signed a peace treaty while the NUR carried on with its dispute, because the union knew how much the proposed changes would affect

One of the converted three-carriage 1960 Craven trains at Ongar before the line closed in 1994.

train crews, station staff and all other departments of London Underground.

The District Line converted its trains to one-man operation, and all its guards were transferred to other lines of their choice. Many were transferred to the Central Line, and this caused overcrowding in the canteens because they actually had no vacant positions to fill, since the Central Line was already fully staffed. The Piccadilly Line was next to go over to one-man operation, causing the same problem.

These surplus guards were offered guard jobs on the Northern Line, or promotion to train driver to fill vacant positions on other lines, while those who didn't want to drive trains were offered jobs on the stations. London Underground had to do something with them, because these guards were just sitting idle at depots doing nothing at all for many months.

Soon all lines were going one-man, apart from the Northern Line, which the unions were totally against converting for safety reasons, in view of the deep tube tunnels. At least keeping the Northern Line guards did save any redundancies that I am sure would have taken place otherwise. The Northern Line wasn't exactly the ideal line to work on; with its long dusty tunnels and overcrowding, it was always known as the 'misery line'.

The Victoria Line never had any staff problems because it had been running automatic trains since the line opened in 1968. The drivers on this line seemed very contented, as you hardly ever heard of any complaints about their one-man operation.

All operating staff were now feeling very tense, as the new changes were closing in very fast. Staff became very unsure of their future with London Underground. No one wanted to see the changes take place, because everyone had been contented in their jobs. Why spoil things on the underground, which had been working well for the past 50 years?

In the early 1990s vigilantes known as 'Guardian Angels' swarmed over the underground in groups, wearing their red berets like soldiers as they marched up and down platforms late in the evening. Commuters welcomed them because they felt protected from troublemakers, but London Underground and the British Transport Police weren't so keen, because they gave commuters the impression that London Underground and the Police were short-staffed. Some train crews welcomed the vigilantes, because it saved them from trying to remove unwanted passengers from their trains. They mainly patrolled the Central and Northern lines, which suffered most with troublemakers. Admittedly they all seemed very well trained in removing people and were very quick, never delaying the service in any way. Fights were rare because they worked in groups all the time. After a few years these vigilantes gradually fizzled out for reasons unknown.

London Underground has always prioritised the safety of its commuters, but it was impossible for British Transport Police to patrol every station at once. More CCTV cameras were installed on all stations throughout the network to deter any trouble, and signs were erected informing commuters of the cameras to make them feel safer. Each CCTV camera records on video 24 hours a day, so the police can use the tapes for evidence if needed. Watching too many crime movies set on the American subways is enough to deter anyone from travelling on the underground, with so many scenes of murder and rape, but in reality this only occurs very seldom on any underground system in the world.

The most common trouble for commuters is pickpockets, who scour the underground in organised groups, especially at the busy underground stations in central London. Train drivers have to make announcements over the public address system to warn commuters to keep their personal belongings with them at all times, which does deter the pickpockets to some extent.

Ticket touts are also a problem. They can earn a fortune from picking up used tickets and travel cards from barrier gates, then trying to persuade passengers to buy the tickets at a cheap rate, providing that the ticket is correctly dated so that it can still be used in the barrier gates. British Transport Police are warning commuters not to purchase cheap tickets and are gradually arresting the perpetrators for theft.

Considering the size of the network, in my experience I would say that it is safe to travel on the underground. On the whole crime is very low when you consider how many people travel. London Underground mainly suffers from petty vandalism from youths who have nothing better to do with their lives. I am afraid that is a reflection of our society today, and I hope the next generation doesn't follow suit.

London Underground would be a cleaner environment if alcohol was completely banned, although it would be very difficult to stop passengers consuming alcohol on trains and stations. Drunkenness causes sickness, and the disposal of cans and bottles can be a nuisance. To enforce such a law would mean employing more staff and extra police to stand at every barrier gate throughout the network.

9
MODERNISATION OF THE CENTRAL LINE

In the early 1990s London Underground introduced the 'Company Plan', which took effect straight away regardless of the trade unions. Now London Underground was a company, which meant many new changes. All staff within a grade received the same salary, no matter what shift they were working. Double-time on Sundays was abolished, together with extra payments for working after certain times ('dark money'). Payment for meal relief was also abolished, meaning that staff were at work for an extra half-hour without payment. Remote booking on and off was also introduced, which meant that train staff no longer had to book on and off at their own depot. This move was very annoying because it meant travelling in your own time, making the shift longer. Because London Underground wanted to cut numbers, severance pay was offered to long-serving staff, and many train crews accepted it, especially if they only had a very short time before retirement.

Loughton depot was closed to save money, and all train crews were sent to either Hainault depot or Leytonstone without being given a choice. All senior train staff were sent to Hainault, which was very much against my wishes as I used to hate working at Hainault. This was a very sad time in my working life and I was sorry to see our Loughton depot close after many years. The ten sidings at Loughton, which were used for stabling trains overnight, were retained, and Leytonstone train crews were booked to use them on their schedule working sheets.

The Company Plan also affected station staff. Station grades began to change as outside contractors took over all the station cleaning, and Stationmasters became extinct as top managers replaced them. Ticket collectors became extinct when ticket barriers were introduced. London Underground decided to make a new grade on the station side, known as Multi-Function staff, who were trained to cover every aspect of station work, including the booking-office. This grade had the same salary as a train driver because of the responsibility involved. The garden and building departments were abolished as work was now carried out by outside contractors. The track maintenance workforce was cut because Railtrack was put in charge of this aspect for all the underground lines.

Depot working was hit as well. Fewer staff were needed to maintain trains now that depot staff were being trained to carry out various tasks like changing brake pads, changing conductor pick-up shoes, preparing trains for service and working in the shunting cabins, allowing trains to enter and leave the depots by changing the points in conjunction with the signalman. More outside cleaning contractors took over the cleaning of trains overnight, while others took over washing trains in the acid sheds and picking up the litter at terminal stations during the day.

Now 50 years of underground working had changed for all the grades of staff, and it led to widespread unhappiness and low morale. The unions had been defeated after many months of dispute with London Underground. Many staff who didn't want to work under these new agreements resigned, while others took their severance pay and found other employment outside. It was the biggest shake-up in the history of the London underground.

In 1993 my wife and I decided to move from the station house at Theydon Bois because we wanted to buy our own property now our finances had improved, so we bought a new home in Harlow, Essex. My stepdaughters had by now left home, giving my wife and I time for ourselves when we weren't working. My wife also worked shifts as a senior care assistant.

I was missing my work on the Epping to Ongar branch line, because Leytonstone crews now covered this section. Eventually, little used and losing revenue, and after many public meetings and disputes, the line finally closed on 30 September 1994. It was deeply missed, especially by the railway staff who had been working it for many years; they were transferred to other stations west of Epping on the Central Line.

On a more positive note, London Underground decided it was time to renew the train stock on the Central Line, since the 1962 tube-trains were now 30 years old. Three new tube-trains were built by three different manufactures, and a series of trials and votes would decide which was going to be chosen to run on the Central Line. The new trains were displayed in Woodford sidings to give sufficient time to decide.

Once the Central Line tube stock had been selected, ABB Transportation Ltd, the successful contractor, got on with manufacturing the whole fleet of more than 560 units, which were made up to form more than 70 eight-car trains. A lot of high technology was involved, making them quite different from all other London Underground tube-trains.

While our new stock was being built, extensive training began to take place, firstly on the new signalling that was to be introduced for the new trains, which would work under Automatic Train Protection (ATP) and Automatic Train Operation (ATO) only. Block marker boards, white boards displaying a red diagonal stripe and a

The converted 1960 tube-trains used on the Epping-Ongar branch were repainted for their last journeys on the line before closure in 1994. *A. Rodgers*

Above A train of 1992 stock for the Central Line modernisation having just been delivered to Ruislip depot. Many trial runs were made to sort out teething problems

Below The smart interior of the new stock. Most of the train equipment is hidden underneath the seats.

Above The driver's cab of the new 1992 stock, showing the view of the platform displayed on the CCTV monitor.

Below Drivers at Hainault depot being trained in the use of the detrainment ramp for evacuating passengers in an emergency.

track section number, replaced many colour-light signals, and white-light signals were introduced for the very first time, indicating to the driver that there was another train in the section ahead before the next coloured signal. For old trains not fitted with ATP, the white signal was treated as a red danger signal for safety reasons. Fog light repeater signals were taken out of commission, because trains running under ATP and ATO didn't need them. All these changes and much more were to take place in the very near future once the new tube-trains were ready to enter service.

More training on the new trains took place and I must admit that it was very hard to understand at first. Many aspects of the train equipment, compared to our 1962 stock, were completely different, including the braking system. There was no longer the train-line air that had been used to operate the Westinghouse brake, passenger emergency handles, and 'dead man's handle', as all of this equipment was now going to be operated by main-line air, apart from the Westinghouse brake, which was done away with.

The 'dead man's handle' was to be replaced by a traction brake controller attached to the driver's armrest on the comfortable armchair seat and serving as a brake. The driver's cab was much larger with buttons to operate the passenger doors, monitors for platform viewing, and information regarding train equipment defects. Handbrakes would be a thing of the past, because the new braking system would be capable of holding the train on any gradient without air leaking from its brake cylinders like on the 1962 stock. Small miniature circuit breakers (MCBs) replaced the fuses, making electrical defects easier than ever to deal with. All this modern equipment was designed to ensure that the driver didn't have to leave his cab as often as before to isolate equipment.

While all this training was taking place on the Central Line, a new control centre was being built at Wood Lane. This would cater for the new trains and signals, because at a later date all the signal cabins were to be closed and replaced by track loops and computers to upload and download train information. New computers were also being installed to control signals, so that trains could run at the correct times and be held as necessary according to the state of the service.

Passenger platform destination describer boards were being replaced by matrix displays giving information on the state of the service and the exact time and destination of the next three trains scheduled to arrive at the platform.

The Central Line guards were now getting very worried about the forthcoming appearance of the one-man trains. Many were offered promotion to train driver, as more would be needed. Those who refused either applied to fill vacancies on the Northern Line or became station assistants.

By 1995 our new trains had begun to arrive at West Ruislip depot, although it took many months before the last unit was completed. ABB staff had to carry out intensive tests on the trains before they were allowed to run in passenger service, and were only allowed to run them from West Ruislip to White City during non-traffic hours to sort out the teething problems that occurred.

Tunnel sections had to be widened to cater for the new stock, especially on sharp curves. Small sound barrier ledges containing asbestos had to be removed from the entire Central Line tunnels. Other new projects involved the renewal of track, especially at crossovers, which were lengthened to allow trains to travel much faster over the points. Meanwhile the new signals and block marker boards were put into place all along the Central Line, including the Hainault loop.

Once all the work had been completed we were ready for the new trains to run. At first only the West End crews were allowed to drive them, because initially they only ran from West Ruislip to Northolt, to do the final tests for teething problems. Meanwhile the East End crews were still receiving their vital training and passing their examinations on the new stock, to be followed by intensive stock training and a road test for every driver on the Central Line.

Finally, when the new trains were allowed to travel eastbound to Epping and Hainault, we had old and new trains running together. The new trains made the old stock look very

A train of 1992 Central Line stock leaves Liverpool Street station. Note the matrix display beside the cab, which gives information on the state of the service and the exact time and destination of the next three trains due to arrive.

shabby and dirty, with the graffiti blending in with the dull silver paint. Gradually the old 1962 stock was scrapped, a few examples replacing the 1959 stock on the Northern Line. It was a very sad sight to see our old trains disappearing after so many years of reliable service to passengers and crews. Perhaps I felt this sadness more than most, because these trains were only four years old when I had first joined London Transport and I had grown up with them throughout my career.

As I was driving one of the last 1962 trains on the Central Line, once again a passenger decided to jump in front of me. As I arrived at the platform I saw a male passenger run from the subway and dive under my train. I had managed to apply the emergency brakes straight away, because I could see his intentions before he took his last dive. Before switching off the traction current I had to walk down the platform, looking underneath the train to see what carriage he was under. When I discovered he was under the fourth carriage and presumed dead, the traction current was switched off for the emergency services. My guard and I carried out the emergency procedures to make it safe for the emergency services to retrieve the body from beneath my train. After an hour's delay I had to drive my train to White City to be relieved by another driver, who took the train to West Ruislip depot for examination. Once again I was interviewed by the police and breathalysed to ensure that I was free of alcohol. Once I arrived home I just burst into tears and remained sick for the next three months.

While on sick leave I volunteered to receive counselling from London Underground every week. I felt very strongly that I needed this to overcome my shock and get back to work, which was what I wanted. My doctor allowed me as much sick leave as I wanted, because she could see how badly I felt from the tears in my eyes every time I went to her surgery. The counselling lasted for at least four visits; each time I was taken to Marble Arch underground station and just stood there, looking into the 'suicide pit' where the incident had taken place; it still contained the sand that had been spread there to cover up the bloodstains. After I had attended the Coroner's court I began to get over my shock and was ready to go back to my job, providing my doctor and counsellor agreed. Once I was given the OK I was soon at work again, although I must admit I did feel a bit nervous at first.

On my first day at work I just couldn't believe my luck. There had been some operating problems on the Central Line and all trains were running late and out of sequence. I happened to be waiting in platform 1 at Leytonstone, while another westbound train was waiting in platform 2; the latter left before me, which meant that it was the other driver who had to deal with the person who jumped under his train at Leyton, the next stop. Without dwelling on this subject too much, I have often wondered since how I would have coped with another shock soon after the last one, if I had been that driver. Many drivers on the underground who have experienced suicides have either resigned or taken promotion to work on the stations.

All depots on all the underground lines have their own counselling groups of train drivers, who are ready to spring into action if a driver needs counselling no matter what time of day it is. Happily the suicide rate on the underground has fallen over the last few years and we are down to only one or two a week throughout all the underground lines.

The Waterloo & City Line, affectionately known as 'the drain', has been in existence since 1898, built to allow London & South Western Railway main-line passengers to reach the City. Before London Underground took over this line in 1994, it belonged to British Railways, which ran a shuttle service consisting of tube-trains. These trains outlasted their working years until the 1992 tube stock replaced them in 1993.

At Bank station the tracks are on either side of an island platform, but at Waterloo it was necessary to use side platforms to leave room for the pillars that supported the main-line station above. There is also a small depot sited at Waterloo used for normal train servicing. Any other work requires the trains to be lifted in and out with a crane so that they can be transferred to another depot.

Subsequently the line was taken over by the Central Line, with Leytonstone drivers the only ones allowed to operate it. There was some talk that the Central Line needed the Waterloo & City Line trains to make up the stock to run its 30 trains per hour. These were going to replaced by 1972 Northern Line stock, some of which was transferred to Hainault depot to be refurbished and is still awaiting its final fate.

'The drain' is closed on Saturday evenings and all day Sunday. Train drivers never operate on one train throughout a shift as on other lines, because during the peak times the trains are so close together that there is insufficient time for drivers to walk the length of their train to the other cab; instead, each train is taken out by the driver of the previous one. This line becomes very busy in the peak hours as each train is packed full until the end of traffic hours.

Having been working on the Central Line for so long, I decided to ask for a transfer to Lillie Bridge depot to work on the ballast trains. These are operated by battery locomotives, which are only used for engineering work during the night, when all passenger trains are stabled in their depots or sidings, during the weekends, or in emergencies. Battery locomotive train drivers are trained to serve on all London Underground lines, so this meant plenty of training, which took months to complete. I also had to learn every siding and depot.

These battery locomotives are, as their name suggests, powered only by batteries, because when carrying out engineering work the traction current is switched off, especially of course when new trackwork is being laid. They can also run on an electric feed from the current rails when possible, which conserves their battery power.

One of the Transplant battery locomotives used on maintenance trains. Some of these trains were fitted with ATP equipment to run on the Central Line.

This driver's position paid more than driving passenger trains, and drivers were entitled to more overtime and other extra payments including travelling time. In the end, however, I decided against the move, because of the long distance I would have to travel to and from work, giving me less time at home.

10
NEW TECHNOLOGY

On 20 November 1996 a power cable fault from the main generating station brought London Underground to a standstill, trapping thousands of passengers in their trains for at least four hours. I was on duty that day and was just arriving at Wanstead platform when the power was lost. I was one of the lucky drivers who managed to get into a platform, while others were stuck in the tunnel sections, unable to move.

This power fault affected every line on the underground, causing a mass evacuation for the passengers who were stranded. On the Central Line we were still running with mixed stock; the drivers who had the 1962 stock when the power went off were able to coast to the next station, providing there was a gradient, unless a traction indicator was showing three red lights (the rule states that you must not pass a traction indicator). Drivers on the 1992 stock, however, could only coast for up to 60 seconds before the train applied its brakes automatically.

No passenger was injured during the mass evacuation, and London Underground eventually managed to restore some electricity, but not to all lines. The Central Line was closed for nearly two days until the fault could be rectified. I volunteered to book on duty for a night shift to recover a stranded train at the eastern end of the line together with other drivers who were going to retrieve other trains nearby.

Now the Central Line had said goodbye to the last of its 1962 stock and it was time to test all the new signals and trains on the full line. London Underground had been unable to test this new equipment before, because there was nowhere else do it. Unfortunately the testing had disastrous results, with many train breakdowns and signal failures for months ahead. The Central Line, not the Northern Line, now became the 'misery line'. It lost its reputation, with hundreds of passengers finding alternative routes to and from work to escape the upheaval through which we were going. Other passengers who couldn't find alternative routes had to suffer being trapped in the tunnels and experiencing long delays. Even the staff were unhappy, because the situation was embarrassing them in front of the passengers, resulting in many arguments. Staff had no guarantee that they would finish their duties on time, which resulted in plenty of unwanted overtime. However, we had no other choice until the operating problems were sorted out.

One of the main problems was the track coding, a vital aspect of train running. Providing a section of track was free of other trains, resulting in the signals showing a green or white aspect, a coding would be displayed in the driver's cab on his speed monitor, which would allow the train to run at a given speed, known as the target speed. When a signal failure occurred, this code would be lost and the train would not be allowed to move unless the driver moved his master switch to the restricted position, and even then it would only allow the train to move at a very slow speed, according to the rules.

ATP (Automatic Train Protection) had now been introduced throughout the Central Line, making it very safe, especially for the train drivers, who received audible warnings in their cabs when approaching a red danger signal. The target speed would also drop to zero, allowing the train to stop before the next danger signal.

Once our main teething problems were solved, allowing us to start running a decent service again after many months, our Central Line manager stated that he would never test anything again! He hadn't been expecting this new technology to bring us so many problems.

Wood Lane control centre had by now installed its new equipment for running and controlling the Central Line. Many computers were installed to run signalling equipment, where one signalman could operate all points and signals on the entire line. Once this came into operation signal cabins began to close down one by one until Wood Lane was in charge throughout. Back-up signalling panels were installed at various stations just in case the Wood Lane signalling equipment failed, otherwise the Central Line would grind to a halt.

More brief training was scheduled for us train drivers, to teach us the basics of ATO (Automatic Train Operation), which would allow trains to run automatically without the driver driving and stopping the train. At first I didn't like this idea, because we would not be in control; it was scary to have to rely on the train itself to stop at a red signal, or even stop correctly at the platforms without over-running. This brief initial training involved trackside equipment, where various loops fed information to and from train and control centre, providing train information and instructions. One vital instruction the train received was how many wheel revolutions it would take to stop it in the next station without over-running or stopping short at the platform.

One evening my wife and I visited my parents as I was on my rest day. My mother was her useful cheerful self, and suddenly I looked at her and wanted to kiss her for being such a wonderful mother. However, I never actually did so because our family had never been the type to kiss, not even in greetings or goodbyes. That evening I said goodbye for the last time, because my mother died of a heart attack two hours after we left. Luckily my father was strong, as he coped very well under the circumstances.

After a week on sick leave I returned to work. More signal cabins were closing down and special timetables were being brought in nearly every weekend to cater for engineering work to replace sections and improve the running for our new trains. We drivers got fed up with this special working as it took many months, although at least the new sections of track gave the passengers a much smoother journey than before. London Underground had to build new equipment rooms in every station to cater for the new technology such as the trackside equipment and our future ATO working. All this was proposed for the very near future, and quite honestly I was dreading it.

The depot at Hainault had a very small rest room that catered for at least 100 drivers. The original rest room had been much larger, but had been very rarely used, being a long walk from the manager's office where we went to book on for duty. London Underground therefore decided to erect a new building to cater for train and administration staff, which would make everyone's life easier as we wouldn't have to be walking up and down platforms and climbing stairs. Even the Station Managers were pleased, because their office in the old building had been very small to start with and we train crews hadn't helped by going in and filling up every available space all the time. Some managers used to throw us out, especially if they were busy with paperwork.

When the new building was finished a footbridge was erected, because the new building was on the north side of the station, built on top of the embankment and passenger car park. The top floor was used for administration staff and the top manager, while the ground floor catered for the train staff managers and crew rest room. The latter, which was equipped with a television and computer, was for train crews only, to give us some entertainment during our breaks. The building also had showers, a locker room and conference room.

The White City training centre had now closed for good; not only was the building old,

Above The new staff building at Hainault was built in 1999 giving staff modern facilities at last.

Below Train drivers booking on for duty in the new offices at Hainault. We have to book on wearing full uniform (excluding a tie in the summer months).

The Duty Train Manager at Leytonstone busy keeping the east end of the Central Line running on time.

but also London Underground wanted to sell it to a private developer. Our new training school was located at West Kensington, and was very different from the previous one. It had at least ten extra floors, to cater for all types of training. The train simulator was moved to Hainault depot, allowing all drivers on the Central Line to refresh their training when required. This simulator has two driving cabs, one at each end, to enable two drivers to be trained at the same time. The driver sits in the simulator while the instructor causes train defects by operating switches out of sight. The train driver then operates the equipment to rectify the defects and also uses his public address system, pretending to speak to passengers. Thus the situation is treated no different from a train in passenger service.

Each year we were also required to pass an oral test on the rules concerning signals, the switching off of the traction current in an emergency, the protection of staff, operating problems and track access. Each driver had to pass this examination in order to retain his or her licence for another year. Every few months drivers were monitored by one of the Station Managers, to see how well we were performing both our driving duties and the use of the public address system. These Station Managers normally sat in one of the carriages out of sight of the driver.

Fire training had now been introduced each year for all operating staff; it used to take place at Acton or Waterloo, but was now taken at your home depot. Fire training consisted of watching some gruesome films like the Bradford football fire, showing how fire can spread. We were also taught how to extinguish fires the correct way using the proper fire appliances. This fire training was very important for all operating staff, because we never knew when we might be involved in a fire incident one day. Fires are very rare these days since smoking was banned after the King's Cross disaster, when new safety rules were introduced throughout London Underground.

Basic first aid training was also carried out every year to ensure that staff knew how to give artificial respiration; this was practised on a plastic dummy. We also had to know how to put patients into the recovery position while waiting for the emergency services to arrive if they collapsed. London Underground also held advanced first aid classes every year for staff who wanted to know more about this subject.

My home life began to take a turn for the worse when my wife was rushed into hospital with pains in her chest, although the doctors couldn't find any reason for her condition. My father was in the same hospital at the time, dying of cancer. My manager allowed me one week of special leave to visit them as visiting hours never corresponded with my shift work. I needed time off work anyway, because with all this worry my concentration wasn't up to driving trains.

After a week my wife was allowed out of hospital, although the doctors still didn't know what was causing her chest pains. I returned to work against my will the following Monday as my special leave had expired, and when I arrived at White City station after my first trip another driver relieved me, saying that I had to telephone the Station Manager. To my horror he told me that he had just received a telephone call from my sister saying that my father had died a short while ago. I felt so upset that I just couldn't tell any of my work colleagues what had happened. I stayed at home for another week, until after my father's funeral.

Under the Company Plan, with all the changes it involved, job titles began to change. For example, 'train driver' became 'train operator' because we were now working one-man trains. When I first joined London Transport a train driver was called a 'motorman', but this changed in the 1970s. Nevertheless, I still call myself a train driver, because that is what I am. Passengers were also renamed, becoming 'customers', because London Underground had become a company. However, I still call them passengers, because the dictionary states that this means a 'traveller, especially by public conveyance'.

Once again my wife and I moved, this time to Benfleet in Essex, to a two-bedroomed bungalow 5 miles from Southend-on-Sea. This was going to be my retirement home in another 14 years. Admittedly, I had further to travel back and forth to work, 50 miles a day in my small car, but once I got used to the journey I didn't mind, because it was more or less a straight road, only taking about 40 minutes each way, as long as I didn't go in the rush hour. Provided I had the chance to enjoy the fresh air and my garden, I was contented in my spare time, away from the dusty tunnels and crowds of passengers. Having suffered with asthma for many years, I needed this time away from work.

I decided to buy a computer as I really wanted to use the internet and explore the World Wide Web to find out more about my many interests. When I discovered the chat rooms on one server, I thought it was terrific to be talking to people all over the world, until my wife began to suspect that I was chatting up other women! This caused a bit of an upset at home while I tried to convince her that I wasn't. One day, just as I trying to prove to her that I wasn't chatting up anyone, some female I had never heard of sent me an instant message. It started off 'Dear Rob' and finished with lots of kisses. I could understand how this looked to my wife, but I was totally innocent because people in chat rooms use these expressions amongst themselves. I did make friends with an American lady who I call my best friend and always will. I have no idea what she looks like and I never will unless she sends a photograph, which she has declined to do many times before.

The time had nearly come to end my working life, against my will. One day at work I felt pains in my chest and pins and needles down my right arm. These symptoms only meant one thing to me, that it had something to do with my heart. I booked off duty to visit my doctor before the surgery closed as I was beginning to feel very concerned. I was given an ECG test, then my doctor sent me to hospital for further tests as they couldn't find anything wrong with me. The following morning I went to Edgware Road to visit the London Underground medical centre for more tests. Their ECG showed that there was in fact something wrong with my heart, and once again I was sent to my own doctor to diagnose the problem. He still couldn't find anything wrong with my heart on his ECG machine.

It was decided that I should remain off sick until London Underground could arrange for me to have a heart test. There was a six-month waiting list for this test at my local hospital, so London Underground decided to pay for me to go privately, since otherwise it would have cost them more in sick pay. Within two weeks I took my test, and the results were OK, so I was cleared to continue with my driving duties.

11
OF MICE AND PASSENGERS

The Millennium had arrived and with it more than two million people who wanted to celebrate this special event in London. This was to be the largest people-moving exercise that the London underground had ever tackled, involving local authorities, trade unions, police and other transport providers. Discussions were held well in advance to ensure that plans were made for crowd control. This meant closing down certain stations to prevent severe overcrowding and to ensure that public safety was maintained at all times.

When midnight arrived on Millennium Eve, more than 6,000 London Underground staff were on duty, 4,000 more than would normally have been working at that time. Around 10,000 shifts were completed on the tube during the weekend, as services ran non-stop for 42 hours. It was the first time since the Coronation of King George VI in 1937 that trains had run all night on the underground.

All train drivers on the entire underground were shown a video and received a book and map, warning us of the problems we could expect from the massive crowds, such as overcrowding on trains and the fact that the majority of passengers would be under the influence of alcohol.

London Underground was praised for the way it dealt with the event. There were no reported assaults on staff and only one accident. With so much advance planning, we all did a great job and London Underground gave credit to its entire staff where it was due. After the Millennium the great clean-up began, with thousands of bottles lying everywhere on the stations and trains. This had been expected and extra cleaning staff soon cleared them away.

The New Year began with services returning to normal. The Central Line service was improving with fewer train breakdowns and signal problems, although more engineering work on renewing track was proposed for the weekends. Tons of concrete was poured into embankments to stop landslides and to improve the safety of these new, faster trains. Because they were now being set to run faster, wheel slide protection equipment was fitted to prevent trains from sliding on wet slippery running rails. Soon after this the stock was taken into the depots to have the equipment adjusted so that every train in the near future would run automatically.

To keep the modern underground in fashion, new uniforms were introduced with the aim of making all staff readily identifiable to passengers. Ann Tyrrell Design, a company with a decade of experience in producing high-quality workwear, designed the new uniform, and you either liked it or hated it depending on your taste in fashion. It was certainly very different from the five previous uniforms I had received in the past.

In the years I have been employed on London's underground. I have seen many changes take place: the opening of the Victoria Line in 1968 and the Piccadilly Line Heathrow extension in 1973, the Jubilee Line being opened by HRH the Prince of Wales in 1979, and the Docklands Light Railway in 1987, not forgetting the recent extension of the Jubilee Line from Waterloo to Stratford.

I have always enjoyed being a driver,

although I often got annoyed with passengers who sat in the first carriage behind the driver's cab, as they would often tap on the cab door, smoke cigarettes against all the fire regulations, spill drink that ran into the cab and eat smelly takeaway foods. I also very much disliked trying to remove passengers who were under the influence of alcohol, as they could often become excessively violent, especially if I was abrupt with them.

I was sometimes amazed by what passengers did. For example, it became necessary for time to time to detrain passengers when the train had become unsafe for passenger service (perhaps because of a broken window or some other defect). I have never understood why passengers would moan at me when this happened. If I was travelling on a train or some other form of transport, I would be the first to obey the driver's instructions so as to ensure my safety. Drivers don't do things like that for their own convenience or to avoid getting out of their duties!

I shall always remember the time a passenger fell in between the carriages and got dragged into the tunnel. This incident caused at least a seven-hour delay on the Central Line. At the time I was driving the third train behind and was held in the tunnel with more than 360 passengers on board. Once the traction current was switched off, the train lost all its lighting apart from the emergency supply, which left each carriage very dim. I kept making announcements to keep my passengers informed of the situation, but after an hour the air began to get very stale and the atmosphere humid, and the passengers were becoming very frustrated by the wait. As the train batteries ran down, the train also lost its emergency car lighting, public address system and train radio. Now I felt alone with all these passengers, unable to keep them informed and also unable to follow any instructions from the Line Controller because the radio was not working.

The only thing I could do was to walk through the crowded carriages advising the passengers that detrainment would soon take place, which at least calmed most of them down. When I got to the rear driver's cab, I laid down the short-circuiting device across the current rails as I knew that the traction current was switched off. When I returned to the front driver's cab I was greeted by station staff who helped me put the detrainment ramp down, so we would be ready to detrain once the order had been given to the station staff (as I had no communication with the Line Controller). Once detrainment started, the passengers couldn't get off the train quickly enough. A few women passengers were worried about the tunnel mice running up their legs.

Once detrainment had taken place, I went back and sat on my train, waiting for station staff to bring me something to drink, as by now I was very thirsty. Sitting alone in the dark with only my hand-lamp, I was very pleased when I was invited to wait in the station control room; at least I could drink my coffee in comfort.

I was very pleased that the passengers had stayed calm up to a point. When passengers know that something is seriously wrong, they normally understand what the driver has to go through. Only one woman complained about my actions, feeling that I had not given enough information to her and the other passengers. I tried to explain that this was because I had lost the use of my public address system when the train batteries went flat.

Very often we train drivers would chat about passengers being trapped in the dark, dusty tunnels on our trains. Often one of us would have an idea about a better way to handle the situation, like asking passengers who do not feel well or who suffer from panic attacks to sit in the first carriage near the driver. In reality this wouldn't work if the train was fully laden with passengers. I normally opened the cab door so that passengers in the front carriage could see what was going on. This often stopped panic attacks, especially if I could get into a conversation with them.

Now that all trains are operated by a single driver, this can cause great concern when the train is trapped in a tunnel. There is no one in the rear carriage to stop passengers leaving the train, unless you can find a responsible person to do this.

They say it takes all sorts to make a world.

Well, it also takes all sorts to make up a group of passengers, whether travelling on trains or waiting on platforms. Very often when driving trains, especially if I was running late, I was surprised by how many passengers would look at their watches, then look at me. This body language could be very annoying, especially if the late running was not my fault. Some passengers would stick two fingers up at the driver, while others would put out their arm for me to stop halfway down the platform. I was often amazed by how many passengers would walk down the platform hoping to board the train when I had to stop half-way.

It also takes all sorts to make up the staff of London Underground. In the staff canteens the West End crews would sit at one side of the room, while the East End crews sat on the other. It had been like this for years with no sign of changing. Well before my time, drivers used to sit at different tables from their guards. There was a lot of snobbery between the grades in the old days, with the drivers thinking themselves superior to their guards.

A test train, intended to ensure that automatic working was suitable for the Central Line, had now completed ATO (Automatic Train Operation) tests. All train drivers were sent to West Kensington for three days training, followed by assessments and a final session on the simulator at Hainault depot. Because training couldn't cater for every driver at once, those who had passed their examination were only allowed to drive their trains in automatic mode where permitted, until every driver on the Central Line had qualified. Of course it took quite a few months to train nearly 400 drivers.

Automatic working was only installed on the underground sections, because the ATO technical staff were unsure how the trains would brake on wet running rails in the open air. These new trains were much lighter than the 1962 stock, making them prone to sliding. Further tests had to be carried out, involving technical staff spraying water on to the running rails with hoses. This resulted in trains sliding in about 40 out of 1,000 runs, even with the wheel slide protection equipment fitted. Once again further tests and trials were carried out, holding up the open section running project.

When I was first qualified to operate my train under ATO, I didn't feel very keen. The train was much faster, especially arriving in platforms, and I often thought that it wasn't going to stop at all. It didn't start braking until you got at least half-way down the platform, and if the train was going to overrun, you had no chance of stopping it alongside the platform.

Overruns did happen to some drivers early on, scaring them; also, as long as the train hadn't overrun the red starting signal, the driver would have to continue his journey without opening the train doors in the platform. If he was unlucky enough to pass the red starting signal, he would be asked to change ends so that he could drive his train back into the platform.

Often the train would underrun, stopping short at the platform. This I didn't mind because I could use the master switch to select the coded manual operation, then drive normally into the platform and switch back to automatic for the next station. If the trouble persisted, you would stick with coded manual until the train could be changed over at either Hainault or West Ruislip depots. Technical staff would then deal with the defect.

Central Line tube-trains were now running much faster, in fact too fast for the 1997 timetable. The new timetable was introduced when the whole line was running under ATO, taking at least 10 minutes off the journey from Epping to West Ruislip, and now that signal control was computerised, it was very frustrating to be held at certain stations to keep on time. When you finally arrived at your destination, the train would be dead on time to the minute. In future, the Central Line hopes to be running 30 trains per hour.

Another innovation when our trains were introduced was that passengers could open the train doors themselves and also close them if it was raining or cold. However, after a while the door buttons began to wear out and passengers would be left on the train or platform, unable to operate the doors. This led to many passenger emergency handles being pulled down. London Underground therefore decided that it would be more convenient to let the driver open and close the doors in the 'driver operation' mode – and this was easier for the driver as well.

Each carriage on Central Line tube-trains held two fire extinguishes. Unfortunately, these were also very handy for troublesome passengers, who would spray the water all over the carriages, and often trains had to be taken out of service with wet seats. Sometimes the extinguishes were thrown out on to the track and or embankments from moving trains, which could have caused many nasty incidents. London Underground therefore decided to call in the London Fire Brigade Inspector to certify our trains as safe to run without fire extinguishers, except in the driver's cab, where they were vital in case of emergency. Once the Fire Brigade had completed its test, London Underground was allowed to remove all of them, saving them thousands of pounds each year.

Vandals often pulled the armrests from the passenger seats, and each day at terminating stations they were stacked up high in the rest rooms. Once again London Underground decided to discontinue providing them, and every armrest was removed. Now the latest craze in vandalism is scratching the train windows, and if they become too scratched these large costly windows have to be replaced for safety reasons. As a train driver I get annoyed about vandalism, because there is no need for it.

Sometimes we get children throwing stones at our trains, and when windows are broken the train is taken out of service. I shall always remember seeing a young teenager standing on a footbridge shining a laser beam in my eyes; the police soon removed him after I had reported him. Of course the horrible graffiti is still around, sprayed all over our trains and signals, and on the signals in open sections.

Vandalism is very difficult to detect on trains, because the driver cannot see inside each carriage while the train is moving. If passengers see vandalism taking place, they may not feel safe enough to report it or intervene. Sometimes the less they see, the better it is for them.

Commuting can be a very serious business,

This Central Line train was completely sprayed with graffiti by vandals on Christmas Day when the underground was not running.

especially when people travel to and from work without a glimpse of a smile or a laugh. London Underground staff often make passengers smile by what is said over the public address system. At one station I once heard a member of staff, as passengers were boarding my train in the peak hour, ask people over the public address system to 'move right down in the cars and smile'. I thought at the time he had it right, because who ever smiles travelling on the tube? Often I have said things over the public address system and heard passengers laugh, especially when I get a sentence back to front.

Over the years good and bad buskers have entertained our passengers in the subways, hoping to earn some cash. Often the police would tell them to leave the station as they were breaking the law, and many arrests were made because the buskers returned to their spot over and over again. Sometimes they were left alone, especially if they were talented, because they weren't causing anyone any harm. Eventually, London Underground decided to legalise busking at certain underground stations as an experiment, deciding that commuters wanted to listen to good-quality music as they travelled. These buskers were selected from a wide group as London Underground only wanted the best musicians. In Paris they even audition musicians, and there is good-quality control of buskers on the Metro.

Underground mice have also brought some entertainment as they run along the platforms and track. Many commuters enjoy watching them, especially tourists. London Underground has to put down poison every now again, otherwise the system would be overrun. By contrast, rats are very rarely been seen on underground stations because the food supply for them is limited, although in reality there are a few that scamper through the tunnels, especially in the cut-and-cover underground sections like the District or Circle Lines. They are found mainly on the open sections, nesting in the grassy embankments or in depots.

Pigeons are sometimes found flying up and down on the underground platforms searching for food, having either flown down the escalators from the street or boarded a train at an open-section station. Often when a train is stationary with its doors open, pigeons hop on board, becoming trapped in the carriage when the doors close.

12
TOWARDS THE FUTURE

At long last my two weeks of annual summer leave had arrived, and my wife and I decided to fly out to the Greek island of Zakynthos for some sun. This would be only our second holiday abroad since getting married, because we normally headed for the West Country to visit my two children.

I wasn't looking forward to the flight, because my wife usually gets so scared that she grips my arm tight, like a cat's claw. On the plane, one of the stewardesses invited us on to the flight deck, and I was very impressed by the amount of controls the pilots had to operate, just like I did in my driver's cab. The pilots were very friendly, asking me more questions about my job than I asked about the aircraft.

Arriving on the island we were taken by coach along the dusty, pot-holed road leading from the airport to the town. Twenty minutes later we arrived at our hotel and struggled upstairs with our suitcases. To our horror our room faced a busy main road, which was very noisy, and the balcony looked over the downstairs bar. We tried to change rooms, but the place was fully booked.

Apart from the noise we had a wonderful holiday, lazing around on the beach most of the day. The weather was very hot indeed, almost too unbearable for sunbathing on most days. Luckily, the hotel had its own swimming pool in which to cool off, otherwise we would just have melted!

The Greeks were very friendly and their food, in their fine restaurants, superb and very inexpensive. We made friends with a few English couples while sitting in the hotel bar in the evenings; we had lots to talk about and eventually I had to do a dance in a pair of flippers, for which I won a T-shirt and a bottle of wine. Two weeks passed very quickly until it was time to fly home to Gatwick Airport, to be greeted by rain.

When I got back to work ATO was now operating through Leytonstone to Stratford in the open section, as a trial to see how trains would stop in slippery conditions. Some trains did slide and overrun, especially at Leyton, until they reduced the speed into the platform. When they found that trains didn't slide under those conditions, ATO was introduced to West Ruislip and Ealing Broadway with the train-braking perfect, even in slippery conditions.

One would think that the driver would be more relaxed when driving an automated train. I for one never was, because I often wondered if the train was actually going to stop at the platform. I would rather have had control, knowing for a fact that I could stop on the eight-car mark. If the train decided to overrun in automatic mode, the driver had no chance to stop it on the eight-car mark, because in the underground sections the braking is applied at the last minute.

Admittedly, now I had been driving trains in automatic mode for a year, I haven't overrun a station yet. I have stopped short in platforms, which is far better, because the train can be driven forward when coded manual. Sometimes the train stops automatically in between stations due to a technical fault either on the train or at the trackside. Running in automatic mode, with all this new technology, is supposed to make the driver's job easier and less stressful, but in my opinion the stress factor will always be there, because any form of driving involves a certain amount of tension. Controlling passenger flow by opening and closing the doors, especially in the rush hour, can trigger some stress because you need to ensure that you don't trap passengers in the carriages or doors.

Everyone gets their off days at work. You may have a severe problem at home that is worrying you, or you may be feeling unwell for some reason, or you might just be feeling tired. All these factors can make your working day terrible. Officially, if you are feeling unwell you are not allowed to book on for duty. However, with our late and sickness procedure you have to be very careful not to take too much time off work as this can lead to dismissal.

If any staff member is taking drugs to cure an illness, these drugs have to be confirmed with the London Underground medical centre before drivers can perform their duties. If the driver cannot perform those duties, he may be put on light duties, running errands for the managers, until the course of drugs is complete. In cases of long-term sickness, the driver has to have a certain amount of road training again before he is allowed back at work. If any employees are found to have an incurable illness, very often they are demoted or offered medical retirement, depending on how serious the problem is. This procedure is decided between the person's own doctor and the London Underground medical board.

One early evening in the rush hour I was held at the home signal at Marble Arch due to a defective train in front, which was detraining its passengers on to the platform. Once the defective train had departed I arrived at the platform to pick up more passengers than usual. When I arrived at the home signal at Leytonstone, the Line Controller informed me that the train in front had also broken down and that I could be expected to be delayed until it could be moved.

I had to inform the 600-plus passengers aboard of the delay using my public address system. After 35 minutes I heard someone walking on the ballast beside the train – to my horror a passenger had got off the train in between the carriages, having had enough of waiting. I had to make a 'mayday' call to the Line Controller to get the traction current switched off. I also managed to persuade the male passenger to sit in my driver's cab and wait, because he suffered from claustrophobia. Ten minutes later the same thing happened again with another angry male passenger. This time the passenger ignored my pleas and carried on walking towards the station. An hour had now passed and a third passenger decided that enough was enough and also walked to the station.

My next instruction was to walk to the rear driver's cab, from where I was to drive the train in the wrong direction back to Leyton. My passengers were getting annoyed with all this waiting as they were packed like sardines in every carriage. Just as I explained to the passengers that we should soon be moving towards Leyton, the Line Controller changed his mind, because the defective train in front was now able to be moved. As I started to walk to the front driver's cab, passengers in the rear carriage shouted, 'If you don't move this train soon, we're going to get out and walk!' By the time I had arrived to the front driver's cab, the defective train in front had moved, enabling me to pull into the platform.

With situations like that I find it very difficult to keep giving information over the public address system without repeating myself too much. You have to be very careful what you say without causing upset among the passengers. I always find it best to reassure the passengers by saying 'I will keep you updated'. If drivers don't use their public address system on a frequent basis, passengers become more concerned about what is going on.

During this ordeal yet another train had become defective at Liverpool Street, and thousands of passengers were trapped in tunnels for up to two hours. Before the eventual evacuation took place, many people needed medical treatment, the conditions having been terrible. Passengers could hardly move as the carriages were packed, and after a while the atmosphere became very humid, bringing on panic attacks, claustrophobia and other medical problems.

The defective train at Liverpool Street had to be pushed out by another train. The delay had been caused by the fact that the trains had problems coupling up together due to the curve in the track, which meant that the couplings wouldn't line up properly. Some 100,000 commuters suffered horrendous delays as a major part of the Central Line was shut for nearly four hours.

The fuel crisis hit England more or less overnight. I was very concerned about how I would get to work, because working late shifts I wouldn't be able to catch the last train from Stratford to Rayleigh in Essex. The Government allowed some London Underground staff to have priority buying petrol because of the need to keep public transport services running.

Now I had reached the grand age of 50, my medical – to find out if I was still fit enough to drive trains – was due. I was about 20 minutes late arriving at the medical centre in Edgware Road because there had been a gas leak at Paddington, causing severe disruption to the Circle and Hammersmith Lines, and I had used the Bakerloo Line instead. To my amazement I passed my medical and eyesight tests with flying colours. My only concern was my asthma, although I was receiving medical treatment that would prevent an attack.

My home life was becoming like a zoo, with three dogs, a parrot and various budgies, although the latter were kept outside in an aviary. Then one of my stepdaughters moved in with her two dogs. I must admit that I wasn't very pleased about this, because the bungalow was very small and only had two bedrooms. I had to build a study at the side of my conservatory so I could be left alone with my computer in peace. My wife got annoyed sometimes, as I seemed to spend most of my spare time in my study. She kept hinting that certain jobs wanted doing around the home and garden. However, I did get around to doing the jobs in due course – when I felt like doing them.

During the winter of 2000 ferocious storms caused mayhem across the country, and the transport system was wiped out in many areas. More than half of Britain's rail network was at a standstill with huge sections of the country becoming no-go areas. Before the storms many railway networks had already been running delayed services due to the speed restrictions imposed following the Hatfield train crash in October. The roads suffered with heavy traffic jams caused by fallen trees, making some journeys impossible. Airlines had to cancel about 90 flights in total and storms and high seas affected shipping in the English Channel. Even the London Eye, the Millennium wheel, was closed after six capsules were damaged in the storm.

The underground also suffered, with flooding in a few stations. Lotts Road power station had problems with blocked fans from the River Thames, causing reduced services on all lines. The worst incident was on the Piccadilly Line when a train hit a fallen tree on the track between Osterley and Boston Manor, the driver sustaining leg and back injuries. The accident happened at 5am in the morning, when the driver of the train had just left the depot. At least he wasn't carrying any passengers, because no stations had opened at that time of the morning.

The very next day, while I was driving my train from Bank station to Liverpool Street, a passenger pulled down the emergency handle. When I arrived at Liverpool Street I saw some passengers waving to me to catch my attention. I decided to walk down the platform to see what was wrong, and to my horror found a male passenger lying very still on the train floor. Another passenger looked at me saying, 'If you don't hurry up getting help, you'll need an ambulance as well!' I rushed to my cab to send out a 'mayday' call to the Line Controller, but unfortunately the passenger died before the medics arrived. My train was taken out of service to be inspected by police at Hainault depot.

I was invited to visit Wood Lane control centre, and when I arrived I was greeted with a handshake and a cup of coffee. I was very surprised to see how the Line Controllers operated the whole of the Central Line. Three Controllers operated three sections of the line at once. In front of them a large panel on the wall displayed the Central Line route, showing where each train was on the line. The Controllers each had a computer in front of them and a keypad operating their sections. They were kept very busy all the time as something was always going on either on the train side or at stations.

Now all the signal cabins have closed on the Central Line, it's amazing how three Line Controllers can operate signals and points that once involved nine cabins' the new technology having taken the place of at least 30 signalmen on the Central Line. When you consider the Central's one-man-operated trains, they alone save nearly 400 guards, not to mention all the other underground lines. The Line Controllers do not have control over trains in the depots, those movements being controlled by the depot staff, since there are always trains being shunted back and forth for maintenance purposes.

London Underground had decided to give its entire driver workforce block training every year. This training consisted of service performance, fire training, stock refresher, and an annual test of the rules. This had to be completed by every driver on the underground for licence purposes; it also it proved that you were still suitable to continue your driving duties for another year. At least this training kept us in top form, because you can easily forget things, especially with so much to learn and remember as a driver.

Every year we were allowed one day to learn about Railtrack safety rules regarding signals, overhead wires, telephones and emergency procedures. This new training was for safety reasons, because some underground lines run beside Railtrack lines, and the Bakerloo Line runs on Railtrack metals between Willesden Junction and Harrow & Wealdstone. I have never been involved with or even stepped on to Railtrack lines in all my working life, but one day I might if an emergency crops up and I am nearby.

Silverlink trains share Railtrack's metals with Bakerloo Line trains on the Watford line, as seen here at Kensal Green station.

With so many new changes, London Underground decided to give the system a female touch by recruiting women train drivers. They had already employed some women in the past, but not as many as they wanted. At the time of writing there are only 100 female tube drivers out of a total of 3,000. Without guards these days to take promotion, London Underground can only recruit outside to tackle driver shortages, or offer station staff promotion if they so desire. New recruits enter the service from all walks of life. Some have been in the police force or the medical profession, while some are former teachers with many qualifications who prefer to drive trains instead. It just goes to show that you never know where the next tube driver is coming from!

As this book went to press, agreement on the future funding of the underground was reached on 8 May 2002. The London Transport Board authorised the signing of the 'public private partnership' (PPP) contracts between London Underground Limited and infrastructure consortia Metronet and the Tube Line Group. Metronet, a consortium of 'big guns' Bombardier Transportation, Balfour Beatty, Atkins, Thames Water and Seeboard, will upgrade, replace and maintain two-thirds of the underground, with plans to spend nearly £7 billion on the Central, Bakerloo, Victoria, Waterloo & City, Metropolitan, District, Circle, Hammersmith & City and East London lines in the first 7½ years. Bombardier received the contract from Metronet for signalling and 1,738 new coaches to be built at Derby, with the first due off the production line in 2008.

Balfour Beatty will take on the trackwork and Trans4m – a consortium of Balfour Beatty, Thames Water, Atkins and Seeboard – will carry out the civil engineering work together with refurbishment and modernisation of stations. Tube Lines will be responsible for maintenance and improvements of the infrastructure on the Jubilee, Northern and Piccadilly Lines.

The author at the controls.

The unions will continue to campaign for our railways to be re-nationalised, and for PPP to be scrapped. After events at Southall, Paddington, Ladbroke Grove and Hatfield – and now with Potters Bar added to the list – privatisation has not gained a good name in the long run.

My wife and I often tune into BBC Radio Essex, as we enjoy listening to broadcasts concerning our home county. One morning I was listening to a chat show about books, which was very interesting, and I sent the radio producer an e-mail concerning certain books. Within two days I received an e-mail back asking me to telephone the radio station if I would like to talk on the air. Two days passed while I tried to decide whether or not to do it. My voice was putting me off, because I didn't want to stutter my words as I often do when feeling nervous. 'Oh, damn it!' I thought eventually. This would be the chance of a lifetime for the thousands of listeners who were going to hear me talk! Once I had decided to go ahead I telephoned the radio station and booked an appointment.

When I arrived at Chelmsford in Essex, one hour early, my wife and I decided to have a pub lunch before crossing the road to the radio station opposite. To my surprise I wasn't feeling as nervous as I thought. Once I had been introduced to the producer, I was on air for 25 minutes talking about my long service on the underground and the many experiences I had gone through. I also talked about this book, which I had nearly finished writing at the time.

I had now become a radio star to my work colleagues, as many of them listened to the radio programme. They thought I had done well representing the underground and hadn't said anything wrong. However, I had to take much teasing and comment from them until it was finally forgotten.

Every day, when you book on duty, you never know what sort of day you are going to have. Anything can happen, from passenger action to major operating failures. I know that I have been trained to cope with such incidents, but perhaps our passengers only see their driver as a figure driving them to and from work each day. Since the Moorgate crash and the King's Cross fire, London Underground has tried its hardest to improve the safety rules. Will something like that ever happen again? We all hope we never see a repeat of such tragic disasters, although no one can foretell the future. The London Underground is changing to fit the modern world with new technology to run the tube as it has never been run before.

Since I joined London Underground I have seen many changes, most of them over the last ten years. Before that, nothing much had changed on the Central Line, with our old trains having run there for 30 years. Admittedly, I enjoyed those days more, perhaps because I was much younger – and now I have good memories of the good old days. I often wonder if the tube will be better in future with this new technology? What will become of London Underground when PPP is introduced? All these vital questions will be answered one day in the future.

THE CENTRAL LINE: HISTORY AND OPERATION

The route

In 1891 the Central London Railway was formed to run an underground tube service along the east-west axis of London, connecting the western suburbs to the City. The line that opened nine years later, in 1900, ran from Bayswater Road to High Holborn beneath Oxford Street. The original western terminus was at Shepherds Bush, sometimes known as Shepherds Green, from which a single line ran to a surface depot at Wood Lane.

Central London Railway

TRAINS RUN EVERY FEW MINUTES

From		First Train	Last Train
SHEPHERD'S BUSH	(Week days) ...	5 0 a.m. ...	12 5 a.m.
BANK	,, ...	5 20 a.m. ...	12 30 a.m.
SHEPHERD'S BUSH	(**Sundays**) ...	8 0 a.m. ...	11 30 p.m.
BANK	,, ...	8 20 a.m. ...	11 50 p.m.

Stations from City to . West End

BANK
POST OFFICE
CHANCERY LANE
BRITISH MUSEUM
TOTTENHAM COURT ROAD
OXFORD CIRCUS
BOND STREET
MARBLE ARCH
LANCASTER GATE
QUEEN'S ROAD
NOTTING HILL GATE
HOLLAND PARK
SHEPHERD'S BUSH

Average Time between Stations 2 minutes

In order to ***AID*** *in rendering the Service expeditious, clean, and comfortable for all, Passengers are requested*

To enter and pass along the Lifts QUICKLY

To be ready to leave the Train immediately on arrival at destination

To be careful to extinguish MATCHES, Cigar and Cigarette ends before throwing them away

To refrain from Spitting

To refrain from Smoking in the LIFTS

GRANVILLE C. CUNINGHAM, *General Manager*
125 High Holborn W.C.

An advertisement for the Central London Railway, circa 1903.

At first the line used electric locomotives, but the excessive vibration they caused led them to be replaced by multiple-unit stock; the last loco-hauled train ran on 7 June 1903. There were also two steam locos, used mostly in the depots, to allow stock to be moved without using current rails. At a later date the electric locos were fitted with trolley poles to draw power from overhead wires in the depots.

In 1908, the demands of the Franco-British Exhibition at White City led to the opening of Wood Lane station, built on a loop track with platforms on both sides to save space, allowing the use of the existing depot entrance from the westbound track. The eastbound track was taken under it and the trains ran anticlockwise around the loop.

In 1911 it was decided to build an extension between the Central London Railway at Wood Lane and the Great Western Railway at Ealing Broadway. Because of the intervention of the First World War the work was not completed until 1917, and passenger services did not start operating until 1920. White City station was built in 1947 to replace Wood Lane, the latter having become very awkward to operate now that trains were also running westbound. Wood Lane is used as a depot to this day, without the loop line.

As the new tube progressed, in the 1930s it was proposed to extend the line eastbound to surface at Stratford, where the main line is on an embankment with a bridge over the North London Line. The Central tracks come up on to the embankment, cross the bridge, then immediately dive down again and pass through a tunnel to the edge of Temple Mills yard, where they emerge and connect with what was then the London & North Eastern Railway line to Ongar via Epping.

Construction was interrupted during the Second World War, although the eastern extension tunnels from Leytonstone to Newbury Park were largely complete, and became a factory for aircraft parts; stations were used as air raid shelters throughout the Central underground system. During the war, when the bombs were dropping on London, a crowd crush disaster at Bethnal Green killed 173 people, including 62 children. The extension eventually opened in 1947/8.

The section from Epping to Ongar was operated by steam for eight years as BR, on behalf of London Transport, worked a shuttle until the completion of electrification in 1957. This section closed in 1994 and was sold to Pilot Developments in 1998, who hoped to run trains using diesel multiple units at peak hours for commuter services at other times. Because London Underground uses both platforms at Epping, Pilot Developments was not allowed to use either, and could only run services from North Weald to Ongar.

The Hainault loop line runs from Leytonstone to Hainault and from Hainault to Woodford. These lines are known as the inner and outer rails respectively until the train arrives at Woodford, where it becomes a westbound train.

The two main depots on the Central Line are at West Ruislip and Hainault, and these carry out the maintenance on the trains. Trains are also kept overnight at White City depot and Woodford and Loughton sidings, where they are swept out by outside cleaning contractors and light maintenance work is carried out to prepare each for service the next morning.

Sidings used for shorter runs, especially at peak hours, can be found at Debden, Woodford, Liverpool Street, Marble Arch, White City, Newbury Park and Northolt. These sidings are very useful if a train becomes defective, and can be used to clear the main

Inside Hainault depot workshed. All types of train maintenance are carried out here.

The train wash at West Ruislip depot, through which every train passes before being stabled.

running line as quickly as possible, especially if the train can only run at restricted speed.

Back in my early days in the 1960s signal cabins were plentiful on the Central Line. Leyton signal cabin closed in the 1970s when the crossover to British Rail tracks was removed; BR used to run a staff diesel from Epping to Stratford in the early hours, which was later replaced by London Transport staff buses.

South Woodford signal cabin was closed when the goods yard was converted into a car park, well before I joined London Transport. When I worked on the stations I used to wash the green lino floors in the cabin every week as part of my duties, even though it wasn't in operation.

North Acton Junction signal cabin also closed in the 1970s when the White City cabin became able to control the points. It still stands, however, with its windows bricked in and ivy climbing up the brickwork.

Ongar signal cabin at the eastern end of the Central Line was closed and pulled down in the 1970s. North Weald signal cabin then operated the station starter signal for Ongar, because it would have been a waste of manpower to have employed a signalman to operate one signal every 40 minutes. When North Weald signal cabin closed in the 1980s, Epping then operated the whole of the branch line to Ongar.

When the new Wood Lane control centre came fully into operation and ATO and ATP were introduced, all the signal cabins were closed one by one, starting at the east end of the line. Now the empty signal cabins are losing their appeal, with flaking paint and broken windows, and the signalmen who operated them were sent to other lines or took promotion to some other operating grade.

The stations themselves have been modified over the years in an attempt to keep them looking elegant and bright. Escalators and lifts have been replaced with more up-to-date equipment and station lighting has improved immensely compared with the

A typical Central Line signal cabin at Newbury Park, now disused. All signals are now controlled from Wood Lane control centre.

dimly lit stations of the past. The busier underground stations have been refitted with mosaic tiles giving them a very different look from the old white tiles that some stations still have. The booking hall areas have been fitted with barrier gates instead of the shabby old varnished-wood ticket collectors' boxes.

The open-section stations at the eastern end of the Central Line are more original, still having their original Great Eastern Railway canopies and waiting rooms, except for Loughton station, which was built at a later date. The West End open-section stations do not have the same appeal, again having been built at a later date.

When British Railways (Eastern Region) owned the East End of the Central Line, it built station houses at every station, and it was normally the Station master that lived in them, or other station staff who required accommodation. Even to this day some of the station houses are still rented out to staff, while others are used as Station Managers' offices. Many railway houses built outside station premises have been sold off.

Staff

Over the years the staff's titles have changed dramatically, especially after the advent of the Company Plan. Of all the operating grades the Station Supervisors and station staff have been most often renamed, including Station Master, Station Inspector, Yard Master, Station Foreman, Multi-Functional, Divisional Manager, Area Manager and Duty Train Manager.

Station staff assisting with platform duties and station cleaning, as well as collecting tickets, have also gone through several names: Porter, Railman, Stationman, Station Assistant and Ticket Collector 1 and 2.

Train drivers and guards have also had their fair share of titles: Motorman, Train Driver, Train Operator, Guard/Motorman, Station Guard, Qualified Guard and Guard Shunter.

Other job titles, like Booking Clerk or Signalman, were paid according to their grade, from A to C depending on how busy their positions were. Working on underground stations was grade A, whereas quieter open sections would be either B or C.

London Underground used to employ male or female apprentices to begin their career before they reached 18 years of age. This gave them time to study for whatever grade they had in mind. Most of their time was spent learning at the training school and being sent to different locations to further their working education. They were well cared for, because often they would take part in outdoor activities for awards.

Trains

One of the first tube trains to operate on the Central Line was formed of Standard stock, which continued in service until replaced by the 1959 tube stock, when most units were sent for scrap. Some were shipped to the Isle of Wight to run a service from Ryde Pierhead to Shanklin. Having been overhauled and repainted, they are expected to last at least another ten years on the Island. The London

London underground tube and surface stock

Standard tube stock	Formerly used on the Central Line. Only a few now remain in passenger service on the Isle of Wight
1959 tube stock	Served on the Northern Line until 27 January 2000
1960 tube stock	Only a few examples survive in preservation, and often appear on open days
1962 tube stock	Served for 30 years on the Central Line, after which many units were scrapped while a few lucky ones were sent to the Northern Line, although these were later also scrapped
1967 tube stock	Still serving on the Victoria Line, running automatically
1972 Mk 1 tube stock	Withdrawn from the Northern Line, and many scrapped
1973 tube stock	Still serving on the Piccadilly Line
1983 tube stock	Only lasted for 9½ years on the Jubilee Line
1992 tube stock	Now running, fully automatic, on the Central Line
1995 tube stock	Now serving on the Northern Line
1996 tube stock	Now serving on the Jubilee Line
'A' stock	Serving on the Metropolitan Line since 1960
'C' stock	Now serving on the Circle and Hammersmith Lines
'D' stock	Now serving on the District Line

Below left 1972 Mk II tube stock at Kensal Green on the Bakerloo Line.

Right 1973 tube stock serving on the Piccadilly Line.

Above 1995 tube stock arriving at East Finchley on the Northern Line.

Right 1996 tube stock serving on the Jubilee Line.

Left A train of 'A' stock at Finchley Road on the Metropolitan Line.

Left C69 stock of the Circle and Hammersmith Lines, seen at Barking.

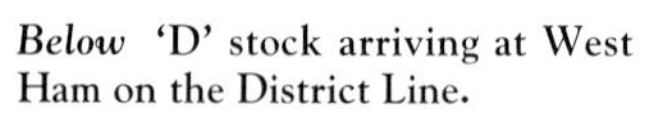

Below 'D' stock arriving at West Ham on the District Line.

Underground museum owns a four-car unit that is now proudly on display, beautiful despite its age, at Acton Museum. Four driving motors are also used for the London Underground maintenance fleet, acting as weed-killing and tunnel-cleaning trains.

The 1959 stock was replaced by the 1962 tube stock on the Central Line, which went on to operate for at least 30 years, proving its reliability. Throughout its working life this stock gave the Central Line a good name with its many thousands of daily passengers. The last run of the 1962 stock in passenger service before it was replaced by the 1992 stock took place on 17 February 1995. Most of the 1962 stock was scrapped, but a few units were kept on the Northern Line, where they supplemented the very similar 1959 stock. These lasted on the Northern Line until a new fleet of trains was received in 1999. Some of the cars from the 1962 stock were saved while others were scrapped. The saved ones were used as Pilot Units and Sandite, Track Inspection and Utility trains. Two units have been preserved; one is undergoing restoration at Hainault depot by members who own it, and the other is at Ruislip depot awaiting a permanent home in which to be restored. The Ongar Railway Preservation Society bought an eight-car train from the 1962 stock, and it was shunted down to Ongar station by a battery locomotive. It stood there for two years, gradually being smashed up by vandals, before being removed by road and scrapped in November 1998.

The origins of Craven Heritage Trains go back to 1994, when the Cravens Preservation Group was formed in order to save the three-car 1960 tube stock. This unit had operated the final day of service on the Epping to Ongar section of the Central Line on 30 September 1994. The Cravens used to run on the Hainault loop from Hainault to Woodford as a shuttle service. They had originally been built as prototypes to replace the pre-war Standard stock that was then operating on the Central Line. Due to the rapid decline in serviceability of the Standard stock and the increase in passenger numbers following the Eastern Region electrification works, it was

This 1938 tube stock at Ruislip Depot has been converted to a weed-killing train for use in the open sections of all underground lines.

Above Withdrawn 1962 tube stock converted for use as a Sandite train. This is used only in the winter months, and sprays a mixture of sand, gel and metal filings on to the rails to prevent wheelslip, and to help the pick-up shoes conduct electricity from the live rails.

Below A train of 1962 stock, owned by Cravens Heritage Trains, undergoing restoration at Hainault depot.

decided that there was no time to thoroughly test the new design. Consequently the 1962 stock was ordered instead. The 1960 units were converted to one-man, fully automatic operation in the 1960s.

The preserved Craven unit is stabled at Ruislip depot, where it was placed by Craven Heritage Trains members in 1997. The unit re-entered service on 27 July 1997 by operating the Metropolitan Line passenger timetable on the Chalfont to Chesham branch. There was another Craven at Hainault depot, but sadly it was scrapped in December 2001.

The 1992 Central Line tube stock was finalised following extensive testing involving three prototype trains from three different manufacturers around 1986. ABB Transportation Ltd built the production version, which features extra-wide doorways with externally hung doors and very large side windows of a type not seen on any tube stock to date. Inside the driver's cab a CCTV enables the driver to view the platform when

Above The preserved 1960 Craven stock at Ruislip depot. Owned by Cravens Heritage Trains, it is only used for railtours.

Right The other Craven train, sadly scrapped in December 2001.

stationary and leaving the station. There is a motor on every axle, which improves adhesion, and braking can be done using tread friction brakes, regenerative or rheostatic brakes, or a combination of all three.

This stock was conceived as two-car units, in which the two permanently coupled cars shared a compressor, shoe gear and thyristor traction equipment. Each train is made up of four of the units, giving it a total length of eight carriages, with a driving cab at each end. Some trains have an extra driver's cab, normally in the middle, but these cabs are usually out of commission due to spare parts.

In the last months of 1998, this stock received a software upgrade, giving each train an increased acceleration and braking rate to enable better performance. Another modification was wheel slide protection, which prevents the wheels sliding on wet running rails and saves them from getting 'flats'. Automatic Train Operation is fully functional on every part of the Central Line, where trains now drive themselves.

Destination roller blinds have been superseded by electronic keypads, where the driver keys in a certain number to obtain the correct destination, duty number and train number. A Data Transmission System monitor in the driver's cab displays train defects, the turning on and off of de-icing equipment, a brake system test and a download system for depot staff to record information for the train file. Fitted to the cab door is a detrainment ramp for use in an emergency.

'Sonia', the digital voice announcer, provides passenger information, stating the destination of the train, giving information regarding interchange stations and telling passengers at which station the train has arrived. The driver can add extra messages by using a keypad in his cab.

The Waterloo & City Line also runs this 1992 stock, which has been painted blue and still runs under conventional signalling. It also still has the trip cock fitted like most other trains on the London Underground network.

The battery locomotives, owned by Transplant, are stabled at Lillie Bridge, the

A train of 1992 tube stock proudly basking in the sunshine at Hainault on the Central Line.

former Piccadilly Line depot at West Kensington near Olympia. There are also some at Ruislip depot with flat wagons to carry ballast and other equipment for track work. These locomotives run on battery power during the night when traction has been discharged after the last passenger train. Some have been fitted with ATP equipment to run on the Central Line, because trip cocks are no longer in use.

The Schoma diesel locomotive (JLF) was bought from the Schoma Company of Germany to assist with the fitting-out of the tunnels prior to electrification. These locomotives were all given female names for some unknown reason, and have been used on various other permanent way projects on systems such as the Epping to Woodford line in 2000.

Above Transplant battery locomotives, used for ballast trains, at West Ruislip depot.

Right A Schoma diesel locomotive built for the Jubilee Line extension.

Driving the trains

Since I began driving trains, I have only driven the 1960 Craven stock, the 1959/62 tube stock, the 1972 Mk 1 stock on the Northern Line, and of course the modern 1992 Central Line stock that I am driving at the time of writing – although it could be said to be driving itself in automatic mode.

On the 1959/62 stock and other convention trains, driving was easy providing you had a control key and reverser key. The control key, which resembled a spanner, was inserted in the control barrel behind the driver; once inserted, the entire train auxiliary circuits would draw 50 volts into the train circuits. With the reverser key you opened up the driver's brake valve isolating cock (DBVIC) in front of you, allowing main-line air to flow into the rotary valve, where it became train-line air. Main-line air was stored in the main-line air auxiliary tanks, and was used for motors, passenger doors, whistle, compressors and the electric brake, known as the EP (Electro-Pneumatic). Train-line air was used for the 'dead man's handle', passenger emergency handles, front and rear trip cocks, and the Westinghouse air brake. As soon as any of these were applied, the brakes would also be applied in an emergency, unless you were using the Westinghouse brake in a service application, when it would be applied gently, releasing the air in stages to the brake cylinders until the train came to a stop.

Modern tube stock still requires main-line air, but not train-line air, because most circuits are computerised, working with very different operating systems. Passenger emergency handles are now designed to warn the driver, not to stop the train as before. The driver will stop his or her train in an emergency or if it is in the area of the platform. Very often the driver will be unaware of the problem until he or she investigates.

Drivers do not need to carry heavy spanner keys these days because on most tube stock only a Yale-type key is required to operate the train. Handbrakes are becoming out of date with the advent of new braking systems, which prevent the train rolling if air escapes from the brake cylinders. Handbrakes were always a nuisance because they were sometimes back-breaking to apply, and the guard had to apply or release the rear handbrake at the same time as the driver in the leading cab. If the train was stabled on a gradient, the handbrakes were also applied in the two middle cabs, together with rail anchors fixing the train to the running rail. There were cases, especially in depots, when trains rolled and crashed into others or the buffers, because train crews or depot staff had not applied the handbrakes properly.

Rolling-stock certainly clocks up some mileage every day, because most service passenger trains run continually all day until the close of service. They therefore have their brake shoes and shoe gear replaced regularly. Depots keep files on all train unit numbers and also download information from the train operating system to find out if any defective parts might need urgent repairs.

Every train driver on passenger service trains will clock up nearly 24,000 miles per year. When I consider my working life on trains, I have clocked up about 720,000 miles so far, so by the time I retire I should have reached at least 1 million miles. Having only experienced two incidents involving suicides, I have done really well considering my mileage to date. I have also done extremely well with regard to train breakdowns, which is a credit to London Underground if you consider how many trains are running at one time. Breakdowns do happen, but not so many as to be really noticeable on an everyday basis. When you consider how many signals are in constant use, some must fail at sometime or other, perhaps if the bulb blows or rodents chew through the wiring, which has been known on quite a few occasions.

Signalling

A railway line without signals would be very dangerous to operate, especially in bad weather conditions on poor visibility, on sharp curves, in tunnels, or with the likelihood of the driver losing concentration. When railways were first built and didn't yet have signals, the railway companies could only operate one train at a time so as to ensure it wouldn't crash into a previous train. When hand signalmen were introduced, it was possible to run more than one train by the 'time interval' method, but this was still not safe, and the hand signalmen weren't always reliable.

When fixed signals were introduced the railway companies were finally able to operate a full and safe train service. Every signal was operated from a signal box or from a ground frame beside the track to allow train movements between signalling sections or into sidings and depots.

As time progressed, colour-light signals were introduced, which were more visible than the traditional semaphore signals. These could only be worked by electricity, which on the underground came from the sub-stations, which fed current into the running rails at about 10 volts. Each section of track was divided into sections for each signal, isolated by a block joint inserted in the running rail. Providing another train was not occupying the section ahead of the signal, it would remain at green. Once a train passed the green signal and block joint, the signal would return to danger until the train was clear of that section. This method proved particularly safe for the London underground, because it ran a frequent train service.

Train stops are located near signals to prevent trains passing them at danger. When the signal is at danger the train stop will be in the upright position, so the trip arm beneath the train will strike it, resulting in the train's emergency brakes being applied. If the signal is clear, the train stop will be lowered clear of the trip arm.

Shunt signals were introduced to allow trains to move on subsidiary lines, such as to and from depots and sidings. Years ago drivers christened these 'dollies'. They are easily recognised by their small circular shape, with a red horizontal stripe on a white background. The face of the signals turns through 45 degrees to allow the driver to proceed. More recently these have been replaced by fibre-optic shunt signals, which look similar to the old type.

Junction route indicator signals were introduced to allow the driver to see what direction the points were set at a junction. These used to show three white lights ('harbour lights') indicating the route, but these have since been replaced by an arrow.

Rail gap indicators are sited near sub-stations; these are triangular in shape and display three red lights that are illuminated when the traction current is discharged, warning drivers not to pass them under any circumstances. If a driver takes his train past one accidentally, he must continue until the complete train has passed it. If the train stops half-way, it will be feeding electricity through

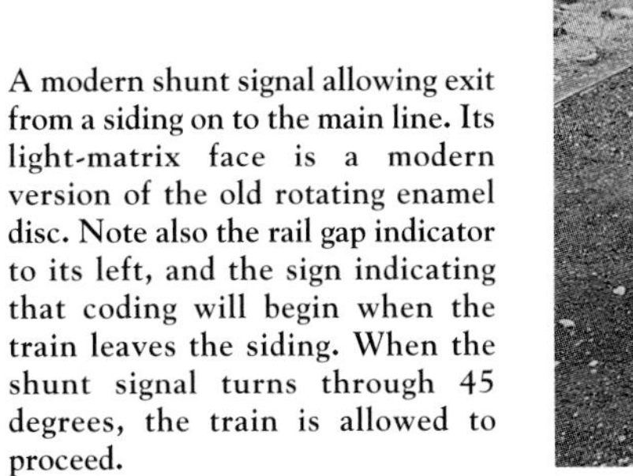

A modern shunt signal allowing exit from a siding on to the main line. Its light-matrix face is a modern version of the old rotating enamel disc. Note also the rail gap indicator to its left, and the sign indicating that coding will begin when the train leaves the siding. When the shunt signal turns through 45 degrees, the train is allowed to proceed.

Above A semi-automatic signal with a route indicator arrow showing that the points are set for straight ahead.

Below A block marker board used on lines where ATP and ATO are in operation.

its wheels and the dead section of rail will be alive.

For the new signalling on the Central Line, block marker boards were introduced for ATP and ATO working. These are treated as a semi-automatic or automatic signals, apart from the fact that there is no visual light. Permission to pass any signal is only granted by the signal controller at Wood Lane or a Station Supervisor. All colour-light signals are operated from Wood Lane control centre by signalling computers, which, together with other high-technology equipment, hold trains in stations until their correct departure time.

Timetable working

The Central Line is now running the number 56 timetable, but this is to change very soon because the line is now fully automatic and journey times are therefore shortened. Timetable 56 was introduced in October 1997 for the 1962 stock.

Timetables are devised at the timetable office at 55 Broadway. Every train running as booked for passenger service has to be scheduled to correspond with drivers' running duties from different depots and sidings.

More trains depart from the depots and sidings in the morning because they have been maintained and cleaned overnight. London Underground doesn't run trains through the night because of maintenance work. Some trains go back into the depot after the morning peak hour, because service requirements are reduced slightly until the evening peak. The Central Line runs 72 trains throughout both peak hours, but after the morning peak this is reduced to 45.

A few selected trains run from White City to Liverpool Street, so as to keep a frequent service operating throughout the central area off peak except in the late evening. Epping to West Ruislip and Hainault to Ealing Broadway trains operate about every 10 minutes. In the City commuters therefore only have to wait a few minutes before the next train arrives.

Most commuters waiting on the eastbound platform at Leytonstone do not understand why more trains go to Hainault than Epping, especially in the peak hours. The Hainault line serves Newbury Park/Hainault/Woodford/Hainault depot, while Epping trains serve Loughton and Debden mainly to be turned short of their journey.

Special timetables are introduced when engineering work takes place, at weekends or on Bank Holidays, and for special events like football matches or the Notting Hill Carnival. Many years ago the Central Line used to run a special timetable on a Thursday to cope with late-night shopping.

Safety working rules

Every member of staff working for London Underground must know the rules concerning safety for themselves and the passengers. Without these rules horrific injuries or death could result. Every member of staff in active operations must pass an annual test on the rules to ensure that they are up to date at all times.

Refresher training is also undertaken every year, involving fire training, train defects and emergency procedures for train drivers. Station staff are also given the fire training, since their responsibilities cover the station escalators, lifts, barrier gates, obstructions on platforms and, of course, the passengers.

All operating staff must know how to switch off the traction current in an emergency, either in a tunnel or an open-section station. There are many reasons why this procedure might be required, such as a person jumping under a train, a track fire, arcing, passenger action, and detrainment.

Signals form a major part of the safety rules for drivers, because of the practice of passing them at danger when they fail. This involves taking the correct procedures to pass them at a caution speed once permission is obtained, and ensuring that all points are secure and facing in the direction of travel before going across them.

Care must be taken to protect workers who need to carry out maintenance on a single track or tube tunnel when trains are running. These workmen are only allowed in for a maximum of 5 minutes at one time to carry out essential repairs, because otherwise they would delay the service.

Care should also be taken when

disembarking passengers from a train in a single-track tunnel, ensuring that the traction current is switched off, short circuiting-devices are positioned at each end of the train, and the detrainment ramp is secure.

If a train overruns a platform, the driver receives instructions from the Line Controller, ensuring that it is safe to drive back into the platform or carry on to the next station.

Care should be taken when staff have to walk the track alone and find themselves approaching a limited clearance area. Access sighting and walking time must be taken into account before walking through the limited clearance area. Care must be taken when crossing the track and stepping over current rails, making sure never to cross where points are involved. When walking through depots there are many potential hazards such as moving trains, shed pits, shed leads, equipment at track level and points operated from ground frames. All staff must only walk on the pathways or walk boards to avoid incidents, and are required to wear a 'hi-vis' vest.

There are more safety rules on London Underground railways than anyone could imagine. Incidents can happen to staff when they break these rules, especially when they are trying to take short cuts to save time. Admittedly, staff incidents are very rare these days, because staff face disciplinary action if caught. Staff also observe the safety rules to protect passengers, who often ignore their own safety by walking on the track, standing too close to the platform edge, obstructing train passenger doors, walking between carriages while the train is moving, and being under the influence of alcohol.

Vandalism has increased over the years and is now at its highest ever level, causing much damage to railway property. This stupid, mindless action can cause death or injury to staff and passengers, whether travelling on a train or standing on a platform. Throwing stones at train windows causes a lot of damage, and they are very expensive to replace. The glass in train windows shatters as a safety precaution, and the train has to be taken out of service at the next station for safety reasons.

Permanent-way staff working on the track at West Acton on the Central Line. The wearing of 'hi-vis' vests is only one of many safety rules to protect them. R. *Millhouse*

Graffiti is sprayed on trains, station buildings and signals in the open sections. This can be cleaned from the trains, but not from the buildings, which stay marked for a long time and lose their architectural appeal, because graffiti looks ugly at the best of times. Graffiti sprayed on signals can be very dangerous, obscuring the driver's view.

Removing fire extinguishers from station premises and trains is another stupid and mindless action that could cause injury or death if a fire was to break out. Some passengers still smoke cigarettes on trains and platforms against all safety rules. These careless people should be reminded of the King's Cross fire, which was caused by someone smoking.

Railway companies throughout England are updating their safety rules all the time, to improve standards and ensure that lives are not put to risk. Perhaps the railways will succeed in this up to a point, but trains will never be 100 per cent safe until they manage to stamp out vandalism and carelessness among passengers and staff.

Underground facts

- When you travel on the underground in the peak hours, you normally discover that whatever line you are travelling on is very busy. The busiest line on the system is the District Line, carrying more than 180 million passengers each year over its 40-mile length.

- The longest continuous journey on the underground without changing trains is on the Central Line, where a journey from Epping to West Ruislip covers just over 34 miles.

- The longest journey by tunnel is on the Northern Line, more than 17 miles from Morden to East Finchley via the City.

- The shortest line on the system is the Waterloo & City, only 1.38 miles long serving just two stations.

- The shortest distance between stops is on the Piccadilly Line, Leicester Square and Covent Garden stations being a mere 0.16 miles apart.

- The highest point reached by the London underground trains is at Amersham on the Metropolitan Line, which is about 500 feet above sea level.

- The lowest point on the system is just south of Waterloo station on the Northern Line, where the tracks are 70 feet below sea level.

- The deepest part of the system is also found on the Northern Line, where below Hampstead Heath the rails are more than 220 feet below the ground. Hampstead station is also the deepest station, its platforms being 192 feet below ground level, and reached by the deepest lifts on the system, descending a full 181 feet.

- Other interesting facts about London's underground concern disused tunnels and stations; in the 1980s a search party tried to find an old tunnel at Crystal Palace, which had been filled in supposedly with a train still in it. Rumour has it that this train was being tested but failed to impress the railway company. This search was soon abandoned, because water made digging impossible.

INDEX